Invisible

to

Invincible

Dawn D. Milson

ISBN 978-1-64492-708-3 (paperback)
ISBN 978-1-64492-709-0 (digital)

Christian Faith Publishing, Inc.
832 Park Avenue
Meadville, PA 16335
www.christianfaithpublishing.com

Printed in the United States of America

I dedicate this book to my children, grandchildren, and to the future generations to come.

I pray each of you will carry on this new legacy of using your voice to bring about change in the things you are passionate about.

Contents

Part 3:   Becoming Invincible

Acknowledgments

Thank you *Nick,* the real love of my life, for showing me what true love is. Thank you for loving me and letting me love you!

For Joshua, Bryan, and Tiffany, the three children God blessed me with. I love you more than life itself. The hard years we have walked together have only grown our love for each other. I hope each one of you never doubts my love for you. Each one of you is strong and courageous despite having all fought our own battles. I am proud of each one of you. We are a team, we dream together, we fight our battles together, and we never give up on each other. I thank each one of you for your love throughout the years and the courage each of you have shown by telling me to write my story. I know this isn't easy because it is your life as well. But we all believe that by sharing our life stories, more lives can be saved.

To each of my grandchildren: I love each of you with everything inside me. I want a better life for you and yours. This legacy of abuse ends here with the generation before you. We know better now. We each have a voice. This family no longer lives in darkness. God is light and the truth sets you free. Not one of you will have to hide. I pray each of you never lose your voice. You stand up for what is right and never forget your love for God, family, and others.

This new legacy begins with you! Carry it proudly and remember who you are. Live your best life and never stop dreaming. Always put God first, forgive others as God has forgiven you. Show kindness and love to others. Now go live your dreams and remember, Nana loves you!

Arlene Gale, my coauthor without whose knowledge and encouragement this book would not have come to completion. Thank you for walking with me during this journey. It was hard, but through the grace of God we did it.

Sheila and Randy Addington, thank you for your spiritual leadership from the time God led me to your door for my first small group. Each of you has poured into my life and Nick's. Your prayers, friendship, and confidence I could move forward with in my purpose in life had helped me become all God has created for me to be.

Peary and Debi Wood, my brother and sister-in-law, thank you for your belief in me and this cause. Peary, thank you for helping me relive our past by retelling the stories in this book to help change future legacies and for reviewing contracts. Thank you both for your financial help with this book. I pray God blesses you many times over.

Lauren Brants, my niece, for your help with edits, research, and encouragement. My sister, your mother, would be so proud you are part of changing this legacy.

Thank you to my friends—*Cathy Gaines, Debra Gikas, Debbie Herndon, Dusti Scovel, and Jennifer Leigh Jones*—for taking hours of your time poring through my manuscript editing and reading content. By doing this, you have poured into my life as well as others.

To all of my clients who listened to my stories while I wrote this book and who encouraged me to keep writing. Thank you!

Thank you to Highridge Church for your spiritual leadership and always pouring into others in order for each of us to find God's purpose in our life. Pastor Dawn Klingenberg, for being a spiritual giant and allowing me to share my story at the women's conference in order to bring about change and hope for others. Many lives have already been changed because of you and this event.

Mission Granbury, thank you for pouring into our community to raise awareness for domestic violence, for allowing me to speak and share my story in order to help awareness bring hope and raise funds so the shelters can provide more victims with safety.

Mary Flores (Crime Victim Liaison Hood County) and *Shelly Muncy* (Victims Services Director for Mission Granbury), my friends and partners in the Enough Program. Thank you, Mary, for your vision as the founder and for inviting Shelly and I as cofounders in order to raise awareness and create change in our community and other communities that are joining our efforts. Thank you for standing beside me during the writing of this book and for your feedback and encouragement as the days wore on.

Mary Pike, thank you for introducing me to Arlene Gale and for listening when God was using you to bring us together. I didn't know the first step in writing a book, but you were the thread that brought this book about. Many lives will be changed by your act of obedience and kindness.

To my Mother and Father, I love you both. We went through hard times, but each of you gave all you knew how at the time. Our bond has never been stronger.

Part 1

Enough

Chapter 1

Enough

I will not cause pain without allowing something new to be born, says the Lord.

—Isaiah 66:9

That night, he knew he'd crossed a line he couldn't uncross. Jack and I had been married for thirteen years, and he had beaten and tortured me throughout the years, sometimes nearly to death. Never before had he directly threatened the lives of my children...but that night, he did. It was a huge mistake on his part—*the* biggest mistake anyone could ever make: he threatened to kill my oldest son. When he was finished beating me in the head, kicking me in the ribs with his pointed cowboy boots, I was left lying in the corner of my kitchen floor, a bloody mess. He knew it was over. Deep down inside, Jack knew his reign of terror; the years of abuse and control over me were done. More importantly, so did I.

The word *beating* seems so insignificant; far too small a word to fully describe the pain so unbearable, death would have been a welcomed choice. In those last brutal moments, I prayed that God would make the torture stop, but I never prayed for death. My children needed me, and I desperately wanted to survive and watch them grow up.

I often prayed for Jack, praying first for God to touch his heart, change him so he could become a better person, the person I fell in love with, and the man I knew he could be. I prayed hard for God to take away Jack's desire for the drugs and alcohol. After years of praying for Jack's transformation, I found myself praying that God would simply take him, keep him from taking the next breath. I desperately, passionately prayed for the answer to the answer to these prayers, so I could survive.

Some people might think the word *beating* is overly dramatic, but this man who swore on the Bible to love, honor, and cherish me all the days of our lives, had turned into someone I didn't recognized, and it was devastating. So much of the day-to-day survival during this time was a haze. Getting out of bed on many mornings, physically battered, bruised, and emotionally drained was not unusual. Getting through every day was a mental challenge I can't even put words to. Worry and fear were my constant companions—guilt, shame, and unworthiness smothered me. So much of the day-to-day survival was a painful blank haze.

Jack worked hard to control me and convince me the beatings were my fault and I deserved them:

If I had only come home on time…or earlier.

If I didn't look at him *that* way.

If I hadn't done ____.

If I'd only done ____.

If I were better at ____.

If ___ (fill in the blank with the theme of the day) was in place, then ___ (fill in the blank with the abuse of the day) wouldn't have had to happen.

On *that* night, the night that would change our lives forever, the smell of meatloaf still filled the kitchen air long after the children had eaten. I remember the details so vividly even now, more than two decades later, they're as clear as if it were yesterday.

It was a Thursday night in the middle of March 1993. Spring had not quite shown its face in north Texas. As is often the case for a Texas spring, it is warm one day and cold the next or feels like winter in the morning and summer in the afternoon. On this evening, a breeze blew softly through the back kitchen door of our small white frame house, cooling down the kitchen that had warmed up during the afternoon sunshine. It was small, less than nine hundred square feet, white with chocolate brown shutters, three-bedroom, one-bath. The living room was tiny, but the kitchen was surprisingly large. It was a tight fit for a family of five with three growing children, but I worked hard to make it our new home.

This house was about one-third the size of our last house. We had just moved from a 2,200-square-foot, four-bedroom, two-bathroom brick home, with hopes that living smaller would help us afford to keep a roof over our heads, the lights on, and the water running.

I earned a decent living and had a good job that I liked. I was making a good enough living to support my family, which wasn't the problem. Jack being strung out on drugs and alcohol again was the real problem. He stayed drunk or high on a daily basis, and in order to support his habits, he was stealing every dime I earned. He even stole the kids' money.

Jack's stealing was so bad, I had to ask Josh, my oldest son, then fourteen years old, to hide the tip money he earned working as a busboy at the restaurant where I worked as the manager. Josh worked nights and weekends to earn his money. He was looking ahead, planning to buy his own car when he got his driver's license by the time he turned sixteen. But when Jack needed money, and I didn't have any left, he went into Josh's bedroom and went through his things to find any money hidden there.

Yes, Jack was so desperate for his next fix that he stole money from my son to feed his drug and alcohol habit while Josh was working hard in school and the restaurant.

For a long time, I covered this up for Jack, because I didn't want my son's heart to get broken. As his mother, I was trying hard to protect his innocence. At least, that is what I thought I was doing. I know now my children walked through the years of abusive hell right along with me. I thought I was keeping my beatings a secret to protect them and maintain the appearance of a "perfect family." I found out years later they saw and heard far more than any child should ever see or hear in their own home. It breaks my heart to know my children saw Jack beat up their mother on a regular basis. My silence hurt us all.

For a little while, I took money stashed away for the rent and replaced Josh's stolen money before he knew it was gone. But there came a time when I didn't have enough money to replace Josh's money anymore. I couldn't keep the sham going. Jack was spending more than I could replace to support his drug and alcohol habit.

It broke my heart, but I had to tell Josh what was happening. I pleaded with him to hide his money in a different place.

One more shattered dream in a long line of hopes and dreams shattered by domestic violence.

On that cool spring night, once again Joshua, Bryan, Tiffany, and myself, finished dinner without Jack. Honestly, I think all of us were relieved. At least we weren't all sitting around the table trying to eat and hold our breath at the same time. We weren't sitting on the clichéd fragile eggshells, not knowing what we might do or say to set Jack's violent temper off. We never knew what mood he would come home in.

After dinner, the kids did their homework. They took baths and got ready for school the next day. Then we sat in the small living room to watch a television program before bed. We enjoyed hanging out and being together.

I looked over to see our dog, Chopper, an English mastiff, laying there peacefully. He was very protective of me and the children. It was his great love for us that saved my life on another night not much different than this one.

Chopper came into our lives when he was only seven weeks old and could fit into my lap. He grew up at a fast rate and never realized he had grown too big to sit in my lap anymore…and he never quit trying. One day, I was laying out in the backyard trying to soak up some sun while the kids played, and here came Chopper barreling around the corner and crawling right on top of my belly and flipping us both out of the lawn chair. We were a heap on the ground with the cheap old lawn chair landing on top of us both. The memory still makes me laugh.

On a previous night, Jack was screaming at me and about to grab me by the throat when he froze in his tracks. I thought, *Finally, I'm getting through to him. He's going to listen to me.*

Time seemed to stand still as I prayed Jack was going to listen to reason. But after what felt like several minutes, Jack was still just standing there not moving or speaking. I looked into his eyes and saw something I'd never seen before—fear. Through clenched teeth, he quietly whispered, "Don't move." I stood silently, a cold chill running through me. I followed his eyes downward and realized where the fear was coming from. Chopper, the now two-hundred-pound mastiff, was slowly circling Jack.

The sound of the big dog's steady toenail clicks and the heavy thud of his paws against the floor echoed off the walls as Chopper's circled. Slow. Steady. Intentional. Protective.

Chopper's back was hunched up and every move was purposeful as he circled around Jack. Chopper never broke eye contract with Jack either. I could see the muscles in Chopper's back ripple and tense. Chopper was clearly sending a message that he would attack if Jack moved a muscle. Chopper could have killed him at that moment.

I remember a passing thought, *Let him do it.*

But instead I calmly called Chopper to my side, "Momma's okay, Chopper. Stop Chopper. Come here, Chopper."

Chopper came and sat between us. Muscles still tensed. Still glaring at Jack.

It was Jack who growled the order: "Take Chopper outside."

I didn't want Jack to hurt Chopper, so I rubbed the dog's head and hugged him to calm him down. I kept whispering in his ear, "It's okay. Momma's okay. It's okay."

Chopper finally calmed down enough to go into the backyard when I called him out.

Jack didn't touch me again that night. Chopper saved me from that beating on that night. However, Chopper would not be able to keep saving me. From that night forward, Jack made sure Chopper was always outside before he hit me.

Back to the life-changing night in question. It was about 9:30 and time to get the kids in bed. After making sure all the children were settled into bed for the night, I ran a hot bath to sit, soak, and relax in. It was getting late, and I was praying Jack would be in a good mood when he finally walked through the door. On the nights he stayed out late at the bars, I never knew what his mood might be and how his coming home would end for me.

The gut feeling I had tonight was it wasn't going to end well, but it was getting late, and I needed to get some rest. Off to bed I went. I'm not sure if I really went to sleep or not, but at about two o'clock in the morning, I heard the front door open. I laid there pretending to still be asleep, hoping Jack would just go to bed. Then I heard him in the kitchen opening cabinet doors.

He's probably rummaging for something to eat, I thought to myself.

All of a sudden, I started to hear him cussing at the top of his lungs and slamming cabinet doors shut.

I jumped out of bed and ran into the kitchen.

"What is wrong?" I whispered to get him to calm down and be quiet so he didn't wake the children.

Instead, Jack started screaming at me, "Why did you throw away the mousetrap?"

"I didn't want to touch the dead little mouse that was caught in it. I wrapped the whole thing in a trash bag and put it in the trash can."

He started screaming again, *"That was so stupid. You are so stupid!"* He sprinkled in a lot of cuss words directed at my lack of value. Outraged at me for wasting a mousetrap I should never have thrown in the garbage. He had gone crazy with rage. He had an insane wide-eyed glare with pupils too small for such a dark room due to his heroin use. His breath smelled like old liquor.

He was completely out of control. Fully lost his mind. Screaming at the top of his lungs while slamming cabinet doors: "I can't believe you threw away that mousetrap!"

Mind you it was a one-dollar mousetrap, but I didn't dare say a word or move a muscle. I stood still and prayed his anger would run its course quickly and I could go back to bed.

In the middle of Jack's tirade, I heard something else. The sound came from behind me. I froze. Dared a glance. My oldest son, Josh, was standing a short distance behind me.

He screamed, "Dad, stop! You promised! You promised you would never do this again."

A look of increased rage went across my husband's face. A look I was very familiar with. I didn't dare turn my back on Jack, but I did take a step backward, moving closer toward my son to shield him. Fear beyond anything else I'd ever felt rose up in my chest, making it hard to breathe. I never had to fear for my children's lives before. I never imagined the day would come where I'd have to physically protect my child.

On many occasions, after Jack would yell at the children, he'd sit down at dinner and apologize, "Dad's not going to do it again. I just lost my temper."

At this point, I wasn't scared for myself anymore. I turned my back on Jack, looked into my son's eyes, and begged him to walk away. "Please, go back to bed, Josh."

Josh didn't move.

I held my gaze directly into his eyes and said, "Son, please do it for me. I need you to turn around and walk out of this room. I'll be okay if you will turn around and walk away."

I was scared because Josh had never taken a stand like this before against Jack. His bravery might get us both killed. But Josh broke eye contact with me and stared at Jack. It was a cold stare that Jack returned.

Both of them stood their ground, but otherwise neither one of them moved to back off.

I quietly and calmly pleaded again, "Josh. I'm begging you. Please. Please. Please! Walk away."

Both Josh and Jack held their ground for what felt like a long time, but then my son turned and slowly left the room.

As soon as Josh left the room and was safely out of sight and sound, Jack grabbed me by the throat, threw me into the cabinet, and started choking me. With his eyes glazed over, giving me a look as cold as steel, he said through clenched teeth, "If he ever confronts me again, I will kill him! Do you hear me? I. Will. Kill. Him!"

My blood ran cold with fear and anger. The life of one of my children was threatened. I vowed to myself: *Never before! And never again! Enough! I. Had. Had. Enough.*

Jack threw me down onto the floor, released his choke hold but kicked me with his pointed cowboy boots. He continued to kick me in the ribs and in the head over and over and over again.

I learned long ago not to scream. It did no good. Sometimes I think it encouraged him to keep beating me and hit harder. Instead, I silently curled into a ball and took the beating. I tried to protect myself with my arms as best I could as he kicked me and threw punches. The pain was shooting through my whole body, but this pain had become my new normal.

I lay there getting the air kicked out of my lungs and having trouble catching my breath, but knowing it was going to be over soon.

This is the first and *last time he would threaten my child,* was the thought that fueled me through this beating.

I would find us a way out.

I would do it to save my children.

Even if I got killed trying.

After Jack made sure he got his point across with the beating, he pointed at me with his face covered in an expression filled with hatred and murderous intent. He looked deep into my eyes and without a word I knew what he was saying. It was a warning and reminder not to cross him or he would kill me and my children.

With one last kick to my ribs, he stumbled off into the bedroom, leaving me bloody on the floor.

Chapter 2

Looking Back

It is during our darkest moments that we must focus on the light.

—Aristotle Onassis

I lay very still on the cold floor for a few minutes to make sure Jack wasn't coming back. Then I pulled myself up off the kitchen floor as I had done many times before. I washed my face. Took some Tylenol. Crawled into bed.

I wasn't sure at this point how I was going to do it, but somehow, I had to find a way out of this situation. I again vowed to get my children to safety, even if it got me killed in the process. As long as my children were safe, that was all that mattered to me. My primary goal was no longer to watch them grow up, but rather it switched to my being able to protect them, with my life if need be, so they could actually have the chance to live, to grow up.

Jack had tortured and beaten me too many times to count throughout the years. However, he had never directly threatened the life of one of my children before, but neither one of my boys had spoken up like this either. Now as the boys were getting older and braver, they were speaking up to try to protect me. These actions would peg the needle beyond the danger zone.

As I laid in bed trying to get comfortable despite the bruising, fear rose up in my chest. I was sick to my stomach. Now both sons had come to an age where they not only knew, but were vocal about, exactly what was going on. The night's beating showed me they were not going to take it and be quiet much longer. This terrified me.

My silence was not keeping my children safe. In fact, I was yet to fully realize how my silence was causing great damage to my children in what it was teaching them and the legacy my silence was creating. I had to find a way out for all of us. Desperation began to battle with fear to take control of me.

However, my husband knew me very well. He knew he had crossed the line and there was no way for us to come back from it. Two days later, he came home, walked through the front door, and pulled all of the phone cords out of the walls. From there, he snatched me from where I was standing in the living room, pulled me by the hair, and jerked me into the kitchen where he grabbed a butcher knife.

He dragged me down the hallway into our bedroom, yanking me by the hair onto our big king-size bed. He started piercing the butcher knife into the top of my skull.

I was terrified.

As angry as I'd seen him before, this level of out-of-control rage went way beyond that.

This time I was screaming.

I was begging for my life.

He held me down on the bed by straddling me. I couldn't move.

The tip of the butcher knife slowly pierced into my head.

I reached up and grabbed the knife. I could feel the blade cutting into my fingers as I tried to push it away. I tried to keep it from moving any deeper into my scalp.

Jack was screaming at me. I felt the tip of the knife push deeper into my skull. "You'll never leave me! I'll see you dead before you live without me. You'll never disappear with the children. If you try, I'll kill every member of your family, one by one, until you come out of hiding, starting with your niece."

I cried. Begged him to stop. I still held the knife's blade tightly for fear if I left go, he would finish plunging it into my head.

He continued screaming, *"If you leave, I will track you down!"*

"Stop. I won't leave," I cried, trying to convince him.

But he kept trying to push the knife deeper into my head.

But he repeated, "I'll kill each person in your family until you come out of hiding. There will never be a place on this earth that I can't find you."

I kept begging, "Jack, please stop. Don't do this, please. Please! Don't let the children come home and find me dead in a pool of blood."

He screamed again, "Never forget. *If you leave, I will find you!* I'll kill you. I'll kill everyone you love. You'll never live without me. That's a promise, not a threat."

I could feel the warm blood coming out of my fingers. But I grabbed the blade tighter, trying to keep the knife out of my head.

I couldn't let my children come home and find me dead or dying.

If I was dead, who was going to raise my children?

How would anyone know that when Bryan put his little tongue in his cheek, it meant he was nervous or afraid? Who was going to talk to him, find out what was wrong, and calm his fears? He needed his Mama to do that.

How would anyone know that when Josh's eyes glazed over, he was tired—really, really tired? When this happened, he was done for the day and couldn't take in anymore. Who was going to tuck him in and kiss him good night? He needed his Mama to do that.

How would anyone ever know that when my little Tiffany was acting so brave and strong on the outside, there was a little girl being crushed on the inside? Who was going to hold her and calm her fears? Who was going to assure her everything was going to be all right. She needed her Mama to hold her and whisper this message into her ears.

My resolve became stronger. I felt a surge of strength I never knew I had. If I couldn't save myself for my own sake, I'd do it for my children.

No one was going to raise my children but me!

I made a decision right then that whatever it took, I was getting out of this situation alive.

Today I was going to live. Live another day to see my children, to be their mother.

At that moment, I felt blood begin to run down my arm. It occurred to me to start doing what Jack loved best. I started stroking his ego, "You know how much I love you! You know I would never leave you. Whatever it takes. We can make this marriage work."

His grip on me and the knife began to loosen.

He started to listen to me. "Let's forget this ever happened, Jack. You know all I want to do is just move forward."

It must have been what he wanted to hear. He wanted to know there was hope for us and that his threats had worked. He began to move.

"Let me off the bed so I can go get Tiffany. My sister is expecting me to pick her up from that birthday party. You know if I don't go pick up Tiffany when they expect me to, Deby's going to know something's wrong."

There was a brief flash of panic in his eyes at the mention of my sister Deby's name. Jack knew she was the one person who had the power and connections to help me disappear if I ever broke my silence.

He started to move off of me but did not fully move away.

"Please, Jack, you know I'm never late. Please just let me off this bed. Let me go get our daughter. Then we can start over like nothing ever happened."

All at once, he let go of my hair, dropped the knife, pulled me up off the bed, pushed me out of the bedroom, and told me to clean myself up.

"Go get Tiffany," he said. "You've got one hour to get across town—and back. Don't be late."

I knew the threat was real. Jack meant every word he said. And he would have my boys at home while I went to get our daughter.

*****

Looking back on my life, honestly, the threats and beatings weren't anything new in my life with Jack. Not long after he convinced me to move in together, he started throwing things at me when he got mad. He blamed his failures, bad moods, anger, and everything else that was wrong with the world on me. He terrorized me until I gave him all the money I earned and had hidden away to pay the bills and buy food. Jack made a good living but spent all he made on his habits.

I always wondered why Jack started treating me so horribly, so violently once we were officially together. I didn't realize at the time that the love and attention he poured all over me constantly was really control and obsession.

I felt like this change in him must be my fault. With me second guessing myself, it was easier for Jack when he told me it was indeed all my fault. Since his family seemed normal, from what I could tell, and he didn't treat any of them badly, I guess it must be me doing something wrong that made him act so violently like this.

Everywhere we went, Jack charmed everyone. When he entered a room, people would flock to him and were glad to see him. He seemed very well liked and seemed to like everyone else as well.

I only knew that, for some reason, I brought out the worst in him. He pushed me into walls, threw chairs at me, cussed and threatened me.

I was pregnant again only three months into our relationship. He was excited. I was excited. I was praying for a little girl to complete our family. But deep down inside, I didn't really think I would have a girl. I had two boys, whom I love dearly, and with two out of two pregnancies being boys, I felt pretty sure I was having another little boy. I would welcome another baby boy. I only prayed for a healthy baby.

As the pregnancy progressed, Jack became more controlling and possessive. It wasn't long before Jack was forcing me to make the drive to the drug houses with him. He was not going to leave me alone. His love had turned to a dangerous obsession, which I didn't really see or understand at the time.

He was always looking for a needle because he was a heroin addict. Once he shot up, he was nicer to me. He'd tell me how sorry he was. He told me how much he loved me. He felt so bad and now that he felt better, he was going to do better.

I didn't understand the drug's role in his declaration of love and his wanting to do better for me. I just wanted his love for me to be true, to be real. I wanted to believe someone could love me.

There were a few key moments in my marriage that I remember very clearly all these years later. For example, in January 1991, only a few days before my thirtieth birthday, when both of my feet were operated on at the same time to remove bunions. My job required me to wear high heels and dress suits every day, standing on my feet ten to twelve hours a day. There were more than a hundred thousand square feet of meeting space at the hotel where I worked, and I walked those rooms and hallways over and over again each day to manage the wide variety of events. At the end of the work shift, I'd take off my shoes and hobble out of the Broadmoor Hotel in pain that was so bad I could barely get to my car.

During the six years I had worked at the hotel, I had advanced through the ranks and had never taken a sick day, but my boss insisted I take the time to have surgery to repair my feet. The projected recovery time was about six weeks per foot. I wanted to have the surgery on both feet at the same time, which was medically unheard of. I had almost enough sick leave and vacation time to cover the six weeks, but that was all. There was no way I could be out of work and without pay for twelve weeks if I did surgery one foot at a time.

Despite the doctor's better judgment, he operated on both feet during the same surgery. The bunion surgery required breaking the bones leading from the foot to the end of each big toe, and then reattaching the toe with screws. I couldn't walk at all due to large bandages. I was sent home and told to keep both feet propped up on the couch in boot casts.

I wasn't allowed to stand or walk on my feet, so I went to the bathroom by scooting on my rear end from the living room to the bathroom, which was about twenty feet away. I'd do my business and then drag myself back over and onto the couch.

It was late at night. The kids were in bed already. I was laying on the sofa in pain when Jack charged into the house. He was drunk and mad about something. When he came into the house, he did so by slamming the front door open against the wall. He was yelling and cussing at the top of his lungs once again.

It all happened so fast. I didn't have time to react. I don't really remember details about how he grabbed my hair, pulled me off the couch, threw me onto the floor, and pinned me between the coffee table and the couch. I just know that he did. Then he started kicking and hitting me while he screamed.

All I could think about was holding my legs up on the couch, so they were elevated and protected. I felt each fist to my head and kick in my ribs, which intensified the foot pain I was already dealing with. The pain from this beating was beyond description. I couldn't escape, crawl, roll away, or curl into a ball for protection because neither of my feet would allow me to do so.

Eventually, after so many kicks and punches, I went emotionally numb. I escaped into my head. I let the thoughts of *Don't panic, it will be over soon* wash over me and somehow provide me with some comfort.

I wasn't going to scream.

First, I didn't want to wake the kids.

Second, I had learned a long time ago to stay silent because if I made a fuss, begged, or screamed, that seemed to encourage Jack in his rage. I said nothing, did nothing other than try to protect my face and body as much as possible with my arms and hands.

I never told anyone about this night. I felt so defenseless as Jack beat me up, but I found out years later my son Bryan saw it all from the top of the stairs. He was so scared. He was only nine years old and didn't know what to do. He stayed silent just like he had been taught—by me. What a dangerous legacy I was creating and leaving behind, but at the time, I had no idea what my silence would end up costing my children. All I knew to do was survive each day and to do what was required from my silence if I wanted everyone else to live.

Chapter 3

Red Flags

It is the Lord who goes before you. He will be with you; He will not leave you or forsake you. Do not fear or be dismayed.
—Deuteronomy 31:8

I know now that isolation is one of the control tactics abusers use. If an abuser can move the immediate family away from extended family members and friends, it empowers them. Isolation is one more way to cause emotional and mental abuse as well as create an atmosphere of boldness for increased physical abuse to continue and escalate. Sometimes the isolation comes from home confinement, and other times it is taking the entire family away to an out-of-town or out-of-state location.

Looking back at my abusive relationship with Jack, I can tell you now the textbook signs of abuse were staring me in the face, including his attempts to isolate me from family to increase his hold over me.

An example of isolating me from others in what was equal to house arrest came after Jack went to work doing exterminating and foundation repair for a friend who owned his own company. Not long after Jack decided we should open our own exterminating company.

The only catch was Jack didn't want to study and take the test for the state license. He promised if I studied and went to Austin to take the test, I could stay home with the children and not have to work again. Sounded like a good deal to me. Jack was excited to do this, so once again I hoped he would find something he loved doing that would add value to his life and keep him off of drugs and alcohol.

"If Jack was happy with his work, maybe that would help make him happy with me again too," I prayed.

I was excited about the possibilities, so I studied for a few weeks, went to Austin, and took the test.

I passed.

"Life will be better now," I told myself.

Well, it wasn't much better.

I did get to stay home, but I was running the company and soliciting business with phone calls every morning, while still taking care of three kids and our house.

Even though the business was going well, Jack decided to move us to Gladewater, Texas, so he could partner with another old friend.

Tiffany was about two years old. Bryan was almost four years old. Joshua, who was ready to start first grade, was about six years old. Off we went to a new town, new home, a place where I didn't know anyone but Jack. This was an example of physically removing us, separating us from my extended family.

We had a three-bedroom wood frame house that sat on a big lot. It had a huge front porch with a chest freezer placed next to the front door. One of my fondest memories is of Tiffany sitting on the porch hoping to catch a wild, little black kitten who was born under the house. He would hide behind the freezer and Tiffany would sit forever watching and waiting for him to peek his little head out.

We also had a pet baby squirrel who had fallen out of a tree. I fed it a bottle every day. We built a cage for him, but he always got out. The minute I came into the kitchen, he ran up my leg and onto my shoulder to tuck himself into my hair. When Josh got up for school, I'd make him a bowl of cereal. The squirrel ran down my arm, sat at the table with Josh, and dipped his little hands into the bowl to eat Froot Loops with him. Finally, I decided to make the squirrel his own cup of cereal.

Bryan and Tiffany would get up shortly after I walked Josh between a row of houses behind us and watched him cross the dead-end street to get to school. When he made it safely into the building, I'd go back across the yard to start the rest of my day.

It sounds like a dream beginning to a new life; however, it didn't take long for things to go wrong again. Jack was back on drugs and drinking.

My worst memory in that house was the day I ran out of money and had no more to give him. Jack needed a fix. We were outside on the front porch. He was screaming at me, telling me I had better borrow some money or find some money somewhere.

Fast.

He didn't care about how or where the money came from. He just wanted the money. Now.

I had nothing to give him, and I had no way of getting any money either.

Then came the worst beating I ever took, or so I thought at that time. I was standing on the porch when he kicked me in the stomach and I fell down to the ground. He continued to kick me in the ribs and head. When he got tired of kicking me with his boots, he rolled his hands into fists and punched me in the head and face over and over again.

Then he stopped. There was silence.

"Thank you, God." He finally stopped.

I stayed still and heard the front door open. Jack walked into the house and I slowly dragged myself up into a sitting position. I was light-headed, so I didn't move much. Blood was rolling down my face and inside my throat every time I tried to swallow.

Jack came back to the porch with a dish towel full of ice.

I thought, *He feels bad now. He went and got me some ice. He's going to apologize and it will be okay. We'll work this out.*

To my horror, he wrapped the ice around his own hurt and swelling hand. It was hurt from beating me repeatedly. Now that he was feeling better thanks to the ice pack, he started beating me in the head again, but with the ice-wrapped hand.

I thought he was going to beat me to death. Finally, he stopped again and left.

I felt the blood running down the back of my throat for three weeks after that. I prayed I wasn't hemorrhaging internally and it would not lead to my death.

Things fell apart in our life again. Jack was driving back and forth to Fort Worth to get his drug fix. He'd spend a few days in Fort Worth and then come back home. He'd leave and I'd never know how long he'd be gone. Sometimes he'd even bring some money home with him from jobs done while in Fort Worth. I was fine with him being gone because as long as he was in Fort Worth, I was safe here. There was peace for me and the children.

Jack had a fight with his business partner in Gladewater, so after a while, we all moved back to Fort Worth. I was so grateful! I was going to be close to my family again. I was back in an area where I knew where things were. Luckily, I never had trouble getting a job. Food and beverage jobs were plentiful.

We stayed in Fort Worth about a year before our next move. Jack was going to try and get clean—again. There was a Christian program in Colorado Springs called the Navigators. These were truly people of God. He did well there and we were happy for a time.

For me this move was a godsend in ways I could never imagine. I was twenty-four years old, in 1985, when I went to work waitressing at the Broadmoor Hotel in Colorado Springs. It was a five-star resort.

The Broadmoor was the prettiest place I had ever seen. It was built in 1918 and stood majestically against the Colorado Mountains with a huge tiered fountain in front of the U-shaped driveway to welcome guests. It is a city within itself: five golf courses, a lake off of the terrace of the second floor, shops, restaurants, a movie theater, and even its own zoo, the Cheyenne Mountain zoo. When I worked there, it had an ice-skating arena where athletes trained for the Olympics.

While waitressing, the food and beverage director saw more capabilities in me. First, he moved me to the catering department to learn the ropes. Then he gave me one of the restaurants to manage. Next, I was put into management in the banquet department. I was the only manager there without a college degree.

When I asked why he was helping me, he said, "Dawn, you have something we can't teach. You know people. You can read their needs. People are drawn to you."

I was surprised and very grateful!

The Broadmoor paid for me to go to school while I was working for them. It was through the Hotel Motel Association that I got my sales and marketing degree. I earned an A in the program and finished with honors. I was so proud.

I stayed with the Broadmoor Hotel for six years. I learned so much during this time. I gained more confidence and had real job skills now. This job set me up for success for the rest of my life. I could write my own ticket anywhere with the background and training I received at the Broadmoor. From here on out, I was able to support my children well and had insurance for them no matter what Jack did.

I will be forever grateful.

Looking back, I see how God put me right where he wanted me. God also had the final say of how far I would go.

Many nights, Jack came home drunk, messed up, or both. On one January night, he pulled the car into the driveway. When he didn't come inside, I went outside to check on him. There he was, passed out in the driver's seat. I opened the driver's side door, shook him to try to wake him up, but he didn't move. I started pushing on him harder, trying to wake him. I was trying to get him to go into the house so he wouldn't freeze to death outside overnight.

I must have pushed him too hard in his unconscious state because he fell out of the car and into the wet snow.

Now what?

Jack was more than six feet tall, and I am five feet two inches tall. He weighed more than 240 pounds, and I was less than half of that.

He was so drunk that when he hit the ground, it didn't startle him. He didn't even open one eye partway. He almost rolled over onto his side as if trying to get comfortable.

I couldn't just leave him there; I was not going to let him lie there and freeze to death.

It was quite an ordeal getting him up off the ground and into the house that night.

Not long after that, I told Jack we needed to move back to Fort Worth. He had no job—again— and my grandmother who I loved dearly had just passed away, the day after my thirtieth birthday. We didn't know at the time I was going to have foot surgery.

The last time I saw my grandmother alive was three months earlier in November. We had come home to Fort Worth to visit and were supposed to stay an extra night, but Jack was so messed up, I was embarrassed. I was scared because I didn't know what he would do, so we left. My grandmother begged me to stay that last night. She was sick and said she would never see me again. My sister assured her she would drive her van and take Mam-Maw to Colorado to see me for my birthday in January.

It is weird how Mam-Maw knew she would never make it or see me again.

In January, mother rode a bus all night in order to come care for me and the kids. She was only there a few days when on January 19, 1991, we got the call telling us my grandmother had passed. She was at my sister's house. Deby was taking care of her while mother was taking care of me. My poor sister did everything she could, but Mam-Maw could not be brought back.

I flew home alone for the funeral in two boot casts about a week after my surgery.

On the flight, I decided I wasn't going to fly home anymore for other funerals. I missed my family. I wanted to be near them. I was getting older and finding myself as a person. I knew God had better for me in life than what I was living. I just didn't know how to get out.

While living in Colorado, Jack had an affair. I was told by other women that he was having affairs. I thought, *They are just jealous of me being married to Jack. They are trying to cause trouble and break us up.*

Then one day Jack came home, showered, and cleaned up after work. He told me he was going south to a friend's house, but when he left our house in my car, he drove north. I called a friend of mine and we went looking for him. I found my car. It was parked at a small apartment complex. I stood outside in front of a ground floor unit, looked through a window, and caught him in the act.

I was hurt and mad. I kicked in the window and went into the apartment. I confronted the coward hiding in the kitchen pantry. This became the next step in a major turning point in my mind.

I went home and got into the shower. I was crying at the end of this horrible night. I was the one who was wronged. I was the one who was cheated on. But he came home furious and found me in the shower. He was screaming at me as he grabbed me and kicked me in the stomach. I fell down wet and crying on the floor of the shower when he left.

As more time passed by, Jack knew he was losing more and more control of me. I could support myself. I had more confidence. This is when he started ruling over me with threats to my family. It was all he had left. He knew I would do anything to protect them. They sure did not deserve the aftermath of what I had gotten myself into.

I was very blessed I had worked for the Broadmoor and doors opened for me back home in Fort Worth. I went to work for the Worthington Hotel when I moved back to my hometown.

I was so happy to be home with my family around. Jack always hated it that my family loved me. He tried to convince me they did not care about me, that he was the only one who loved me and the kids.

Let me tell you: That is not love; that is called control. When they need to know your every move, give you a time to be home, accuse you of things they are probably doing themselves, that is about their insecurities. It is all a mind game they are playing to control you! Love does not hurt, it does not hit, it does not smother.

Chapter 4

The Escape

The name of the Lord is a strong tower; the righteous man runs into it and is safe.
—Proverbs 18:10

I knew the escape was going to happen when Jack threatened to kill my son. He made sure to seal his fate when he put the butcher knife in my scalp. He thought he had won the battle. But Jack had crossed the line. I vowed he would never touch me or threaten any of my children again!

But right now, I had a one-hour time frame to work within until the final escape plan was laid out. One step at a time.

Therefore, with fresh knife wounds across my fingers, a stab wound in my scalp, and a full dose of adrenaline pumping through my body, I ran into the bathroom to clean myself up and bandage my fingers. I grabbed my purse and keys, then ran out to the car where I started shaking because this was the closest I'd ever come to being murdered. I lay my head against the steering wheel and I took one deep breath. There was no time to think about my death right now.

"Pull it together, Dawn," I told myself. "Remember the one-hour time limit Jack imposed had started."

By the grace of God, I was alive right now and able to go pick up my daughter.

I threw the car in reverse and backed out of the driveway trying to breathe, trying to comprehend what happened to me, trying to figure out how I was ever going to get us out of this. The only thing I did know for sure was I was going to get us out of this dangerous mess. I didn't know the who, how, what, where or when, but I was going to do it!

The fear that whispered inside my head right now was "How am I going to escape and keep everyone alive?"

Yes, I thought I might be able to get me and the kids out; I just didn't know how I might be able to keep everybody else in my family safe. I had to find a way out of that house, out of this marriage. There was no doubt in my mind that if I didn't get out soon, Jack was going to kill me, and maybe my children too. And he would kill me sooner rather than later.

As I drove to pick up my baby girl at the birthday party, I tried to put a smile on my face and pull myself together. I didn't want anyone to know anything was wrong. In the meantime, Jack went to pick up the boys. I had to be back at my house within the hour if I wanted all of us to stay alive.

I walked into the party all made up, dressed nicely, and with a smile on my face. Pretending nothing happened. Nothing was wrong. As usual. I said hello to my sister, Deby, and her friend. Deby must have seen something in my eyes, in the stiffness of my body movement. I think she noticed the trembling despite my trying to act calm. Then there were the bandages on my fingers. She knew something was very wrong.

Deby asked, "Dawn, what's wrong? What's going on? What happened to your fingers?"

I smiled and said, "I'm fine. Everything's okay. I need to get Tiffany and go home."

Deby never took no for an answer. She put her arm around my shoulder and led me into another room. She looked into my eyes and said, "I know something's wrong. Dawn, tell me what's wrong."

I couldn't keep silent any longer. I had to get some help. I told Deby the story of what happened earlier. She was so angry. She held onto me and said, "Dawn, you are not going back there. I'm not letting you and Tiffany leave this house."

Now I started to worry.

I begged her, "Please, I have to leave and get home. Please, don't call the police. Don't do anything."

Deby started to protest, but I cut her off.

"He's got the boys," I pleaded. "I have to go back home or risk never seeing my boys again."

I tried to reassure her, "I promise you, I will be safe. I'm sorry, but I'm in a pitiful state right now. I have to go home."

I hugged my sister and added, "Please don't call my house tonight. Don't do or say anything to anyone. Especially don't call the police. If you do, you'll get me killed.

Jack had always told me if I ever called the police, he would kill me and then kill himself before the police could get through the door.

"Deby, he means everything he says. Please don't take my warning lightly. Don't get me killed tonight. As soon as he leaves for work in the morning, I'll call you. We can make a plan."

Deby saw the fear in my eyes and knew I was right. She released me to go home even though she was terrified.

"I want out. I need help. I'll call you as soon as Jack walks out the door in the morning," I tried to reassure her again.

Reluctantly, Deby went to get Tiffany. We left the house as Deby said to me, "I better hear from you by morning or I'm coming over."

Tiffany and I went home as if nothing had happened. When we got home, the boys were already there. Someone who might have just walked in would think nothing ever happened.

Trying to make life seem normal seemed weird after the beating and knifing earlier in the day, but that's what I did, what we all did. I made dinner. We ate dinner. Watched TV. That night, Jack sat smugly on the couch thinking he had won yet again. Little did he know that as he sat there, a plan was being put into motion.

We woke up the next morning, and I sent the children off to school as usual. One of my days off was Monday, so I didn't have to go to work. I tried not to pace impatiently, but I couldn't wait for Jack to walk out the door. I was ready to make a phone call to my sister and get a plan into action. The minute Jack walked out the door and left the driveway, I picked up the phone and called Deby.

She must have had the phone in her hand because she picked it up when it started to ring.

"I talked to Clayton last night and told him the little bit about what we talked about," Deby said.

My sister and her husband Clayton put me on speaker phone. I explained to him how Jack threatened to kill each and every one of my family members if I took the children and went into hiding, starting with their daughter Lauren.

We were on the phone for several hours trying figure out the details, trying to find a way to keep family members safe. They didn't want me to stay at home one more night, but without clear steps on how to get out safely and keep my extended family safe, I couldn't just leave. After going over several different scenarios, but still not having a concrete plan, I assured Deby and Clayton I would be safe at home for the night.

Clayton agreed, "Let's hang up for now. Let me have some time to work on this. But you need to touch base with me in the morning."

It was getting late. I knew Jack would be home soon and none of us wanted him to catch me on the phone talking to my sister.

That night, Jack was in his "I'm so sorry for hurting you" state, which worked in my favor to plan the escape.

The next morning, my phone started ringing. It was Clayton saying he had spoken to his friend who was the district attorney in Fort Worth. The district attorney advised Clayton to take us to a women's shelter because it was the safest place for us until Jack was arrested. Clayton realized this solution didn't help us keep eyes on the entire family, so he hired a private detective. The goal was for the private detective to sit across the street from my house from the moment I called and said I was out. From that moment on, the detective would have eyes on my house and know when Jack came home. Then the police would get called to arrest him.

Now we had a plan for the escape. It was time to start executing it.

Once we hung up the phone, I started my part by calling all the women shelters in Fort Worth. Then the next problem showed up. None of the area shelters felt they could keep us safe in Fort Worth. Jack was from Fort Worth, and they felt he might know where the shelters were located, which endangered the lives of the other women and children already there.

They found another safe women's shelter in another county, but it took a couple of days. It was located in a county just north of where we lived, and it had confirmed space for me and my three children.

The shelter and I devised a plan. When I was ready to leave my house, I would call the shelter to tell them I was on my way. A meeting spot was set up with the sheriff's department, who would send an officer out to meet us and lead us to the shelter.

The next step was to call each of the kids' schools. Bryan and Tiffany were both in middle school and Josh was at the high school. I needed the schools to be prepared and agree to bring the children with all their belongings to the curb when I got there. There was no time to park the car, walk into the school, explain the situation, have someone go get the children, then bring them to the office so we could walk to the car in the parking lot. Time was of the essence once we started the escape.

The most dangerous time for a domestic violence victim is the moment the escape plan begins to unfold and until safely tucked away in a shelter.

I called the middle school first and talked with the principal. We decided as soon as she got my phone call that Bryan and Tiffany would get rushed out of class and taken to the curb to wait for me. They were to get into the car as quickly as possible. Once Bryan and Tiffany were picked up, we'd go to the high school to get Josh.

The high school principal agreed to have Josh at the curb waiting for me when I arrived.

We had to be very careful and detail-oriented, because if my timing wasn't accurate, I would be dead before we made it out of Fort Worth.

During the next two days, while I waited on the women's shelter to get back to me with an answer about where we could go, I needed to figure out where the children and I would live once we left the shelter. We had no idea how long we could stay at the shelter, so I needed to plan what we would do next.

What I did next was something Jack wouldn't think I'd ever do. I rented an apartment in the same complex my mother lived in. Sounds crazy, but I knew Jack would never think about me living close to my mother. He would think I would be afraid of putting her in danger. However, I knew this man well and felt confident he would never look for me there. With my mind made up, I rented a three-bedroom apartment so we would have a place to go once we left the shelter.

I was going to hide right under Jack's nose.

Now for the next part of the plan: It was decided my brother, brother-in-law, sister, mother, and sister's stepson would rent a U-Haul. They were on standby waiting for a call from the detective saying Jack was arrested and we were safely at the shelter. Once these events happened, they would go to the house with the U-Haul and take out all the furniture, our clothes, and belongings, and move everything to the new apartment.

The escape plan was ready to put into place.

I went home that evening and prepared for us to run the next morning. I pulled one small gray suitcase out of the closet and packed it with a few of the children's and my essentials. My heart was pounding as I snuck around the house packing a few things that wouldn't be missed by Jack. I slowly shut the small suitcase and carried it to the boys' bedroom closet and hid it in the far back corner, silently praying it wouldn't be found.

As I looked around at the boys' small bedroom with their bunk beds, navy blue comforters, plaid curtains hanging on the windows, I felt so many emotions: sadness, pain, and fear, and also a glimpse of what hope, safety, and freedom might feel.

I thought: *This is the last time we have to stay in this house. Tomorrow we are going to be free. If we can make it through tonight.*

I prepared dinner as usual, but kept thinking, praying: *By this time tomorrow, if all goes as planned, our lives will change forever. If we make it out alive!*

No matter what I knew, I had to try this escape plan, because as risky as it was, it was a chance to live; it was a chance at safety for me and my children. If we stayed here, my death at Jack's hands was only a matter of time, and then there wouldn't be anyone to stop him from hurting my children. His violence had escalated. He was more and more out of control.

I didn't want to keep focusing on the worse-case scenario. I wanted to think about what was going to happen to take us all to safety. I had no idea the exact location of this shelter. I didn't know what this shelter would look like. But I knew one thing: If we made it there, we would be safe. Tomorrow was going to be a whole new start if we made it to safety.

Do I dare dream about what it will feel like to breathe again? To not walk on eggshells again? Do I dare dream about going to bed at night and feeling safe? Dream about a peaceful night's sleep? Do I dare to dream about creating a safe place where my children can feel safe enough to act like children again? To laugh out loud without worrying if it will make Dad mad? To visit with friends or have friends over without thinking about what happens if Dad comes home screaming and drunk? Do I dare to believe I am the kind of mother who can keep her children safe no matter what?

Yes, I dared to dream about these things and more!

My heart beat a little faster at the thought that this nightmare I lived through for thirteen years might actually almost be over. I took a deep breath.

I kept telling myself, "One step at a time, Dawn. Breathe. Just make it through tonight."

Jack came home that evening for dinner. The game was on. He was not going to stay gone long now. He was going to come home every chance he could because he wanted to make sure I knew he was watching me. His physical presence was another way for him to threaten and control me.

After dinner, the kids did homework, took baths, and headed for bed after watching a little television. Pretty much like usual. But as the boys headed off to bed, I prayed they wouldn't notice the suitcase hidden in the closet, or if they did, they wouldn't ask questions. My nightly routine was to go to each of my children and cover them with kisses and tell them good night. When I got into the boys' bedroom to say good night, I made the decision to tell them about the bag, just to be safe. A big fear was one of the boys waking up in the morning to get dressed and find the suitcase. Then they would ask about the packed bag at the breakfast table with Jack sitting right there.

Jack never left the house before the boys did, so yes, it was best to tell them the secret.

Both of my sons were preparing to get into bed when I walked in to say good night. As I leaned in to hug each of them, I whispered, "There's a suitcase in your closet. Don't ask any questions and don't say a word to your dad about it. I am getting us out of here tomorrow. Get up and go to school as usual, but when the office calls you, you need to get to the curb fast! I will be waiting. We are going to get away from here. I will explain it all when I pick you up tomorrow. It's a new beginning for us."

Each boy smiled and nodded.

One step closer, I thought.

As I crawled into bed, all I could think about was no more sleeping with the enemy. A few more hours and we would be free. I slept very little that night. The plans of the next few hours were running through my head. I was keeping the fear down by repeating to myself, "We can do this. I'll get us all out. All we have to do is make it until morning."

At some point, I must have went to sleep, because my eyes opened before the alarm went off. I jumped out of bed and went into the big old kitchen one last time. This would be the last breakfast I fixed in this house if the next few hours went as planned. I went in and woke my daughter and then woke up the boys. When I woke them, I smiled and put my finger to my puckered lips as I made a soft sound of "Shhh."

Just a few more minutes and the kids would be safely out of this house for the last time too.

Jack was still sleeping as the kids got on the bus for school. I wished he would just wake up so our plan could start unfolding. As if an answered prayer, at that moment, I heard the floor creak as Jack got out of bed. I took a deep breath and held it.

A small voice inside my head whispered, "Act normal, Dawn. Just act normal. You can do this. Everyone's life depends on you."

I let out my breath. My heart pounding. I put a smile on my face as he leaned in to kiss me good morning like there wasn't a problem in the world. Little did he know, this would be our last kiss. Last ever.

He ate breakfast, grabbed his jacket, and headed out the door to work.

I waited until I saw his truck turn the corner. I didn't know it was possible for my heart to slam any harder inside my chest. I grabbed the suitcase from the back of the closet, picked up the phone, and called each school to tell them: "I'm on my way."

Each one assured me the kids would be there waiting for me and the principal would wait with them to help ensure their safety.

The next call was to my sister, "I'm out!"

I hung up the phone, walked out of the front door for the very last time. I didn't look back. There was nothing here for me anymore.

I threw the suitcase into the trunk of my car, jumped in the driver's seat with my adrenaline pumping!

"Please, God, help us all to make it out of this safely!" I prayed out loud.

When I pulled up to the curb of the middle school, the principal rushed the kids into the car. Off I went to the high school where Josh jumped into the car. So far, so good. Now to carry out the second part of the plan.

We met my mother, sister, brother-in-law, and aunt at a Mexican restaurant off interstate Highway 35 headed north. It was about lunchtime and the kids were hungry. Deby took them inside. She explained the plan to the children and made sure they were okay and knew what to expect.

As soon as we got to the restaurant, Clayton rushed me to his car and we headed straight to the district attorney's office to file charges against Jack. The district attorney had arranged to take me around to the back of the building and up the back steps for our protection. They told Clayton a team was waiting for us. They weren't joking. When we arrived, the back stairwell was lined with fully armed police officers waiting for us. Clayton and I jumped out of the car and ran up the back stairwell. A detective took my statement and examined my cut fingers from where I tried to keep Jack from shoving the knife into my head only a few days before.

Charges were filed against Jack for assault with a deadly weapon.

We headed back down the rear courthouse steps and back into the car. It was time to return to the restaurant and get the children. From there, the next step toward freedom included meeting up with the sheriff once we crossed the Denton county line and he would lead us to the shelter.

When we got arrived, the sheriff was waiting just like we planned.

"Thank you, Jesus. We made it this far."

The sheriff escorted us to the women's shelter where we were greeted warmly. We felt welcomed, and safe.

The director showed us to our room, which had two sets of bunkbeds and a dresser with a common bathroom for us to use down the hall.

Being close to my children all night made me feel safe and happy. We were very unsure what to expect here, but so far, I was pleasantly surprised.

I could tell my children were still nervous and a little afraid. Honestly, so was I, but we were out from under Jack's glare, and out of his arm's reach.

I remember going to sleep that night repeating to myself, "We had made it out. We made it. There is no going back."

I still felt unsettled. But for the first time in a long time, I also felt safe and on the edge of allowing myself to feel happy, relief, and hopeful.

Hope was something none of us had felt in a long time.

I was only allowed to use the pay phone in the shelter, which was a secure line. Calls could not be traced.

This might be a good time to remind readers that this escape plan was executed more than two decades ago, long before cell phones. From the shelter's pay phone, I called my sister to see if the private detective had any news to report about Jack's arrest. He was watching my house from the moment the assault charges were filed against Jack, so we would know as soon as he was arrested.

No news yet. Jack had not come home. Everyone was on the edge waiting. The detective was going to check in with Deby again in two hours. At that point, when I called Deby, the report was different.

The news: Jack was arrested as soon as he pulled into the driveway and before he was able to reach the front door. I was told six police officers had him face down. Six shotguns were pointed at his head. He was approached and handled as dangerous, handcuffed, and taken away to jail.

I thought my heart was going to stop when I heard the news.

We had done it! We made it out alive! And Jack was behind bars.

Now for part two of our plan to unfold.

My brother was in a U-Haul truck headed toward my house. My mother, sister, brother-in-law, and my sister's stepson all headed to the house so they could start packing up my belongings. They packed up the household, took everything in it, except for Jack's clothes. Then the truck was driven toward my new apartment where it was unloaded. This part of the plan was falling into place.

We spent two nights in the shelter. Then I convinced my brother-in-law to let me leave the shelter and stay in the new apartment since Jack had been arrested.

As we were setting up the apartment the next day, a call came from the sheriff's department stopped us in our tracks! This was a turn of events we didn't expect.

Chapter 5

More Fear

Fear would have to face the God I know.
—Dawn D. Milson

Every part of the escape plan executed so far had gone as well as anyone could have expected. I took a few moments for a deep sigh of relief after Jack was arrested. Little did I know that a brief moment was all I was going to get.

I'm not sure we knew how the next few days or weeks after the initial escape would play out, but I knew for sure that everyone thought there would be more time to figure out the next steps after achieving the main goal of getting my family to safety. With this done, my heart was happy, three days after we implemented the escape plan, as I was arranging the furniture in our new home, unpacking boxes, and settling us into our new life.

Josh, Bryan, and Tiffany had gone to my mother's apartment to visit. I was looking forward to having the rest of the week off with them because it was the children's spring break. The following week, I was planning on enrolling the kids in new schools.

My mind went back to my boss, who gave me this week off with pay, which was very generous. He had seen Jack come into my office many times demanding money. I was so embarrassed and would hand over all my money just to make Jack leave. When I went to my boss to tell him I needed a week off so we could get away from Jack and explained what was going on at home, he could not have been happier to help. He knew things were bad for me at home, but had no idea how bad it really was.

"Get safe. Your job will be waiting for you when you get back," he assured me.

I loved my job as the restaurant and banquet manager for the Fort Worth Cattle Drive, which sat high up on a hill south of Interstate 30 and east of downtown Fort Worth. It was a beautiful restaurant. The entrance had a huge wood-burning fireplace right before you opened the heavy solid wood front doors. Guests came as much for the food as to visit the iconic longhorn steer named T-bone, who lived in a shelter and fenced-in area attached to the restaurant. T-bone was our official greeter.

Through the restaurant's front doors, toward the back of the restaurant, were floor-to-ceiling glass windows, which provided a grand view of downtown Fort Worth from every angle.

I was part of a hardworking, wonderful staff who was like family. Actually, two of my staff were family. Both of my sons Joshua, fourteen years old, and Bryan, thirteen years old, worked as busboys on some nights and most weekends. They loved making money while being with me.

A big plus for my peace of mind was they were away from the house and away from their Jack.

The boys thought they were rich. Each of the wait staff tipped the busboys each night. If the boys got a ten- or a twenty-dollar bill, they would come to me and asked me for one-dollar bills. They'd roll the stack of one-dollar bills up and add a twenty-dollar bill rolled up on the outside to make it look like they really had a lot of cash in their pockets.

The restaurant staff protected and looked after the boys since they were the youngest employees. Most of my staff were Hispanics who took protecting family very seriously, and to them the boys and I were like family.

On my last day at work before our escape, my boss, the general manager, and myself met with the wait staff to fill them in on what was happening. We felt it was important for them to know because it was likely Jack would come here looking for me. We wanted everyone to know the danger involved and to call the police if he came through the door. No one was to confront him.

If Jack asked about me, the answers were "No idea. Haven't seen her." or "I think she took a few days off."

Now with the employees' safety enhanced, I gave everyone a hug. As I walked out the front door of the restaurant, I looked back over my shoulder at the staff. Fear surfaced momentarily that I may never see them again if the escape plan didn't work. A prayer crossed my heart for the people I had worked with, but also come to love and trust. "God, I pray I am not putting these people in danger too."

Soon I'd find out how much they loved me as well.

The ringing phone brought me mentally and emotionally back to my new apartment kitchen, where I happily began unpacking boxes again. My goal was to try unpacking and settling in as much as possible while the children were with their grandmother.

I picked up the phone and said, "Hello." It was my sister.

My sister didn't take the time for formalities, and with panic in her voice, she asked, "Where are the kids?"

"They are over at Mother's right now," I said, feeling a panic begin to stir inside me.

Deby said, "Dawn, go get them now and bring them home. You have got to stay in your apartment out of sight."

"Why? What…?"

"Clayton just got a phone call. Someone bonded Jack out of jail."

Clayton had Jack's arrest file flagged at the jail so he would know if Jack made bond.

"He is out of jail and no one knows where he is," Deby said. "Get the kids. Get them inside the apartment. Lock all the doors and don't move without calling me first. I'll call you when we find out more."

We hung up the phone.

I could not believe it!

How did this happen?

Why would anyone want Jack out of jail?

Jack made bond, with what money? He never had any money when he was strung out on drugs?

I knew Jack was about to unleash hell on earth on everyone involved in helping me. "Help us, Jesus, please help us! Protect my children. Protect my family, please."

I called my mother's house and told her I was coming over to get the children. She told me not to leave the apartment because the red flag was on me. My mother was sending my younger brother Hershel over with the kids since he had the best chance of protecting them if Jack surfaced while they were between her apartment and mine.

I was told my brother slowed down only long enough to put a pistol in the waistband of his pants. It didn't take long to get the kids back to my apartment. I felt a little bit better because we knew Jack would probably go to my mother's place as a first stop looking for me. The kids were not safe there.

Once the children were safely back inside our apartment, we shut all the blinds, locked all the doors and windows. Then my brother grabbed my car keys, taking the car to hide it somewhere outside of the apartment complex. Hopefully Jack wouldn't see it at all or not think I was living there when he drove by my mother's complex.

Clayton called the private detective and put him back in front of our old house, hoping Jack would go back there and we could keep track of him. For the next two days, Jack didn't go back to the house. Everyone in the family was on lockdown. We knew he was coming after someone in the family. It was just a matter of time.

It didn't take long for my family's phones to start ringing. My sister and Clayton did not pick up the phone; instead, they let it go to the answering machine. At the beep, my sister reported Jack started cussing and screaming at the top of his lungs.

He screamed, *"You better answer this f———ing phone. Now! If you don't tell me where Dawn is, everyone is going to pay!"*

Jack knew they helped me and they were the reason I was able to escape.

"If someone doesn't tell me where Dawn is, I'm going to start killing people," he yelled into the answering machine. "Lauren will be the first! And it will be your own fault."

The way Jack saw things, they had taken his wife and kids; now he was going to take their only child. He'd enjoy watching them grieve for her. If he followed his threatened plan, he'd let them watch him kill mother next. Then he'd kill each one of them if they didn't tell him where we were hiding.

Deby told me later they wanted to pick up the phone and tell Jack that he'd never find us, but they didn't answer. They kept letting his calls go to the machine and get recorded. He called over and over and over again all day long.

Clayton and Deby knew these recordings were evidence of how dangerous Jack was if we ever got him to court. These recordings did indeed do just that and helped save everyone from Jack's threats, or worse.

The next day, Deby went to the courthouse to file for protective orders against Jack to cover the rest of the family: her, Clayton, my mother, Lauren, my brother, and my brother-in-law.

A protective order is different than a restraining order. A protective order is filed in a criminal court while a restraining order is filed in a civil case. Police take restraining orders less seriously because these are filed in civil matters. Because Jack was charged with assault with a deadly weapon, my case was a criminal case. A protective order is given when there is proof of a direct threat to a person's life.

Protective orders were filed and granted by the judge for myself and my children when assault charges were filed on Jack. Now we needed some kind of protection for the rest of the family. My sister presented her case before the judge the next day.

The judge initially denied the orders, saying there was no proof. He wanted proof Jack had threatened all the people we wanted covered by the protective order. Court issued protective orders were very hard to get because most people do not have proof, but rather go to court expecting hearsay to count. But it doesn't.

My sister told me, "I calmly reached into my purse and pulled out the recordings." She told the judge, "I have all the proof you need here!"

The judge took the recordings into his chambers and listened. When he came out, a protective order was indeed placed on every family member on our list. The judge took it one step further by issuing another arrest warrant for Jack. It turned out Jack violated his bond by calling my family and threating me.

With that done, there was a little peace restored. At least if Jack showed up at someone's house, they could call the police and have him arrested. In the meantime, I was worried. "Where was he?"

No one was safe with him out of jail. With Jack on the streets, my children and I were the ones locked up like prisoners.

The private detective reported that Jack never went back to the old house where he was arrested. While the detective watched the house, only his parents went back to gather his clothes and the dogs. After a few days, Clayton pulled the private detective off the case. There was no sense in keeping him parked in front of the house if Jack wasn't going back there.

The week off from my work was gone. The children's spring break was finished. We were all by ourselves during this the week. No one came in. No one went out in case someone was being followed by Jack.

Jack always used the same attorney for all his legal troubles. Because of this habit, we were able to figure out who the bail bondsman was. He told us it was Jack's mother who bonded him out of jail.

After nearly a week of being locked in a dark apartment, I called Jack's mother and said, "I know you paid Jack's bail. I don't think it's fair for your grandchildren to live in fear, in the dark, while your son is running around on the streets. Staying messed up on drugs. And threating my whole family."

I had asked his mother for help before with Jack, but she was in denial about the domestic abuse. She knew he'd been in drug rehab before, but it was not something that anyone talked about out loud. She treated me like I was being dramatic and making it all up. She said, "Jack wouldn't ever hit a woman."

Shortly before we escaped, Jack's violence escalated more and more. One day, she and Jack's father sat in my living room watching television while Jack dragged me from the kitchen where I was cooking dinner, into the bedroom. He was hollering and cussing at me. Once in the bedroom, he punched me several times.

I was begging Jack, "Stop. Stop. Your parents are here."

Jack dragged me by the hair past his parents to get me into the bedroom. There was no mistaking what he was doing to me. There was no way they couldn't hear my pleas and Jack's cussing either. They completely ignored us and didn't lift a finger to help me or stop him.

I couldn't believe it. Jack's dad was more than six feet tall. He could have helped and made Jack stop hitting me, but he didn't. I could almost understand them not believing me over their son when I told them stories in the past, but this time they just sat there in our house and let him beat me. There was no denying they knew Jack was beating me at that time and they did nothing.

It was such a betrayal. I loved them and thought they loved me too. Their lack of help and lack of compassion hurt me more than Jack's beating itself. The beatings at Jack's hands were something I was more used to. I could almost separate my mind and my body from his beatings. But the betrayal by one more person I loved, and in this case, two more people, cut my heart deeply.

Thinking back about this day now, I realize it was one more blow to my self-worth. But still for the sake of my children, I had to try to make her understand what she had done to her grandchildren.

"If you don't keep him locked up when they arrest him again, he will overdose on heroin," I said. "I hope you make the right choice, at least for your grandchildren, the next time."

Then I hung up the phone.

After talking to the police again, there only advice was "Be careful until Jack can be arrested again."

There were not strong laws against domestic violence twenty-five years ago, so unless Jack showed up somewhere he shouldn't be, he wouldn't get arrested. The police were not out looking for him.

We had to come out of hiding. I had to get back to work. Money was tight and running out. Without a paycheck, the kids and I wouldn't have a home.

I was in touch with my job. My boss said Jack called the restaurant to threaten them too. My boss told me, "Jack said if I knew where you were, I'd better tell him or else."

Thank god, they could honestly tell Jack they had no idea where I was.

I went back to work but did not drive my own car. My brother Hershel took me to work and picked me up every day. He was my personal bodyguard. Every day, he packed a pistol and drove me to work. When we got to the restaurant, Hershel stood in front of my passenger's side door and let me out of the car. He walked in front of me holding the pistol at the ready in case of trouble until we reached my office. Then he'd leave and return when my shift was finished no matter what time it was, 11:00 p.m. or midnight on weekends.

All the staff knew what was happening. Every time the big wooden front restaurant doors opened, my wait staff would turn and look at me with a smile on their faces. It appeared to everyone else as if it they were greeting the customers, but it was to assure me all was well. I began to notice when they smiled at guests entering the front door, it was with a hand reaching into their apron pocket.

They were all packing pistols. Every waiter and bartender in the place was carrying protection. I felt safe here. They were not going to let anyone die on their watch!

I had to stop and say a prayer thanking God for the many people who cared for us and were willing to do whatever it took to keep us safe. I felt and saw God's protection all over us.

There was a huge, physical reminder of God looking over me that I saw every day on the drive to work and every time the front doors opened. Directly across about six lanes of traffic that made up Interstate 30, on the north side of the freeway, east of downtown on a hillside, was a fifty- to sixty-foot-tall white cross as an unmistakable sign for me and others in the city that God was watching over us.

The strange thing about the fear I felt going to work with every day was that none of this seemed that out of the ordinary to me. This was my life, and somewhere along the way, I accepted the violence and need for protection as normal. But even during this time, deep down inside of me, I knew God had more for me than this. I was not sure what it was or how he was going to get me there, but I knew there had to be more God had planned for my life.

All I could do now was my part and that meant survive one day at a time.

I spent many hours praying to God and counting on him that this would all work out. I was living on faith.

Looking back now, I can see how God was using these trials in my life to build my faith, strength, and character for the years ahead of me. I can honestly tell you nothing in my life that I can remember has ever been easy. But by God's grace and my faith in him, I have survived it, each step at a time. The good thing I can say about so many trials in my life is that life doesn't scare me or really even make me mad anymore; it is just another step on the journey to help strengthen me for my next mission from God.

The restaurant was only open for dinner during the week and lunch and dinner on the weekends. During the week, I worked in my office. During the day, I was responsible for booking catering events. At night, I felt I had protection. It was the daytime hours that were the most dangerous. My office was up front close to the front doors of the entrance and the only other staff there during the day were a few cooks who came in early to prepare for dinner in the evenings. The kitchen was in the back of the restaurant with no windows, so I was up front on my own during the day.

After about two weeks of my brother driving me everywhere to protect me, I thought something had to change.

Jack had still not gotten arrested, although the threating phone calls kept coming. When I called the police to ask if they had any ideas of what to do because I was afraid at work up front in the building by myself, they were kind enough to come to the restaurant and look at it and help me try to come up with a safety plan. After discussing my situation, the only advice they gave me was to quit hiding my car. Start driving myself to work but be aware of my surroundings at all times. The truth was Jack was going to come after me. The police said I had a better chance of staying alive if Jack found me on my own turf. They told me to have a gun in my office and if he came within arm's length of me to shoot him. It was the best chance at staying alive I had.

The police added, "In most cases like yours, we'll be called back to clean up someone's blood. Your best shot at staying alive now is to do it on your own terms."

With that advice, after going home that evening, I was given a .22-caliber handgun. It would take a well-placed shot to kill Jack; otherwise, it wouldn't do much other than slow him down long enough for me to out if it came to that. No one thought I could handle a bigger gun because I had never shot one before. As of now, the .22 would become my best friend. I would have this pistol with me at all times.

"God, please help me. I'm scared to death but out of options."

Hopefully, I would never have to use the gun, but I would protect myself if I needed to. The advice my mother gave me regarding the gun was "If you pull it out, be prepared to use it. Don't hesitate. If you don't shoot, he will take it from you and shoot you with it instead. He can easily overpower you. Never use the gun as a threat. Pull the trigger." I never forgot these words of wisdom. I knew if things went that far, I would have no choice.

Every day, my new best friend "Mr. 22" and I headed off to work with a prayer that Jack would be arrested soon and this nightmare would finally end. I did not want anyone's blood on my hands.

Every time I heard the front door of the restaurant open, my right hand moved to the pistol laying in my top right-hand drawer that always stayed open while I was at my desk.

Life was going on as usual with the kids in school. Jack had no idea which schools and he didn't know where I lived, so I felt pretty certain they were safe. He was looking for me or my sister, mother, brother-in-law mainly now. Threats came in daily to all of their telephones. Everyone knew by the sound of his voice that when he called, he was drunk, high, or both.

While everyone was very cautious and on edge, life moved forward. A different kind of fear became our new normal.

One day, out of the blue, I received a phone call from my sister. "The police had Jack. He has been arrested."

Jack had to check in with his bail bondsman, and when he did, the police were there waiting to arrest him. The courts would now automatically double his bail, which we hoped meant he'd stay locked up this time.

I had hope this was true. If Jack didn't bond out, we had a few months until trial was set. Maybe we were going to get a break, catch our breath, and regroup.

A quick call to his mother, and I was able to breathe again. I had to ask her to please not bail him out again. I reminded her that her grandchildren's lives were are stake. And that Jack's life was at stake too. He needed time to get off the drugs.

She promised me they would not bail him out of jail again.

"Praise God! We can breathe again."

The only thing we had to prepare for now was trial.

Chapter 6

The Trial

Scars only show us where we have been and they do not dictate where we are going.
—David Rossi

Four months of our new life had passed since we made our escape. We were settling into our newfound life when I received the call from the district attorney. It was time for me to appear in court at Jack's trial. It was only an appearance before the judge as part of the sentencing since Jack pled guilty to a lesser charge of assault with a deadly weapon.

Jack's parents hired a high-powered attorney to represent him or he would have faced attempted murder charges.

In 1993 there were not many laws that protected spouses from domestic violence. Women had few legal rights in cases of domestic violence. The laws that existed then did not provide strong legal protection, and those few laws that did were often not enforced. The court system didn't make it illegal for men to hit or otherwise control their loved ones. Thank God the laws have moved forward to protect victims today.

At the time, I was happy Jack was out of our lives. I just wanted to move forward in peace. Now I think back and wonder if I should have fought for a stronger charge, but the escape and living in fear wore me out physically and emotionally. I was tired of fighting.

There wasn't much fight left in me at this point. I simply wanted this chapter of my life to close.

This was going to be the first time since my escape from Jack four months ago that I was going to see him. My breath sucked in as my high-heeled black pump hit the first step of the downtown Fort Worth courthouse. So many thoughts were racing through my mind at once:

This time I wasn't battered and bruise.

This time I wasn't on the run for my life.

This time I wasn't terrified, cowering and crawling up the back staircase of the courthouse surrounded by armed policemen.

This time I was going up the front stairs and in the front door.

This time I was dressed as a confident woman who was going to stand tall on my own two feet in court, face my abuser, and defend myself.

This time, despite some fear, I was going to take my life back and show him; he had no more control over me.

As my sister and I climbed the tall granite steps one by one, I felt a little fight coming back to me. "You can do this, Dawn. Just a few more steps toward getting justice," I kept telling myself.

I heard a district attorney say once, "For a victim of domestic violence, facing the abuser in court feels like what a snow globe looks like when it is just shaken up."

In other words, when a snow globe gets shaken and all the tiny pieces float in uncontrolled directions, that is what a victim's life feels like. This is what my life felt like at this time.

After a little while, all the pieces in the snow globe begin to settle in place inside the globe's world. This may occur once a victim escapes and begins to feel like she might just be okay again. Then, *bang*. Life gets shaken up by the start of a trial as if the snow globe was shaken up all over again.

My world was being shaken again as one-by-one, my heels clicked up those courthouse steps toward facing Jack one last time. The only comfort was my sister's heels clicking right up the steps beside me. We would do this together. It was going to be hard, but I wasn't going to be alone. My heart raced faster with each step.

I wondered, "Would I still feel free and safe when I saw Jack in court?"

"You are free" was what my heart said to me.

I knew God had my back and I wasn't going in alone. I opened the big wooden doors to the courtroom and stood a little straighter and taller as the district attorney walked toward me in his dark gray suit. He had a reassuring smile on his face as he led me into the courtroom.

Our case was called.

A side door opened and Jack was brought into the courtroom once everyone else was in place. He was wearing the bright orange county-issued prison pants and shirt with the words *Tarrant County* stamped on the back of the shirt. His hands were cuffed in front of him.

When I saw him handcuffed like this, I was both relieved and saddened. I was relieved momentarily because he was restrained, but still I knew if he wanted to get to me, he would. But then, I was sad too because he had wasted his life. The dreams I had for us were never going to come true. I wasn't going to get my happily ever after with this man, maybe not ever in my life. I loved this man at one time; I worked tirelessly to try to get him off drugs and to save his life. But I couldn't make him do it; no matter how much I loved him, I couldn't do that for him.

My sister and I were sitting a few rows from the front of the room facing the judge. We were sitting directly behind where Jack was standing with his back toward us. I willed myself to sit up a little straighter in my seat.

I will not let him see fear in me if he looks this way, I thought to myself.

The judge was sitting in his black robe saying his name and reading the charges against him, and Jack couldn't resist one little turn of his neck to stare directly at me. His glare was as cold as ice.

You know the saying "If looks could kill"?

I knew that look. If Jack got what he wanted, he'd come across the benches, reach over, and kill me. It was the look I had grown used to during the past thirteen years. I sat up even straighter. I never flinched or looked away from Jack's gaze. I was bound and determined that he was going to know he didn't control me anymore.

The judge warned Jack, "Turn around. You will keep your attention on me at all times or else."

When Jack returned his glare from the judge to me, the judge called out to him again, "If you don't do as asked, I will lock you back up and the court will not proceed with the sentencing."

Jack didn't seem to care.

Four more times during the sentencing, he would turn to stare me down, trying to try to put fear in my heart.

I kept telling myself things like:

"He will not win this time."

"I am out from under his control and I never have to go back!"

"It is my choice. I am in control."

"Jack can't force me to do anything anymore."

Each time the judge banged his gavel and called Jack to order, the bailiff in the courtroom moved a little closer toward him. By the end of the hearing, the bailiff was standing directly behind Jack to block him from turning to look at me. The bailiff was literally breathing down Jack's neck; he was so close. If Jack tried anything, he and the bailiff would collide.

My attorney had counseled me before he presented Jack the plea they were offering. It was up to me to agree on what the offer would be of two options. First, I could choose one year in prison. Or I could decide on giving him ten years of probation.

Initially, I thought prison was my safest bet to keep him out of my life, so my children and I would be safe. However, the attorney told me if we chose that option, Jack would probably never serve any more time because he had spent four months in county lockup already. The county gave prisoners credit of three days for every one day served in lockup. Using this formula, Jack would end up with time served and be out later that day anyway.

My attorney felt it was safer for us to go with ten years of probation. This sentence meant that for the next ten years, if Jack came near me or threatened me, he would automatically go to prison to serve whatever remained of the ten-year sentence.

The judge read Jack's plea deal and gave out the sentence. I could feel myself breathe again. It was over. He could no longer control or manipulate me. I had faced my greatest fear with my sister and God standing right beside me.

On this day, I learned "Fear would have to face the God I knew."

Fear is from the devil, but faith is of God. I had faith he would keep me safe, faith he would deliver me. And he did. Fear would no longer control my life.

We won!

Jack still had no idea where I lived, and the district attorney assured me when the trial was over, I would have plenty of time to leave before Jack did because it would take time to process him for release. The district attorney would make sure Jack was held up longer.

I felt a little freedom as we pushed open the big wooden doors to leave and walk down those courthouse steps to freedom. About the third step down, I heard a lady shouting my name. My sister and I stopped, turning around as this lady grabbed my arm. With tears rolling down her cheeks, and a look of fear in her eyes, she said, "You don't know me, but I work for the courts. I was in the courtroom during your hearing. I sent the note back to the bailiff, which is why he went to stand behind Jack."

With full-blown tears running down her cheeks, she pressed a piece of white paper with her name and phone number into the palm of my hand. Her words would bring fear to me once again as she said, "Call me if you need help. I could lose my job for this because I am not supposed to have contact with you. But I hope you know that man wants to kill you! I saw the look in his eyes. Everyone on staff in the courtroom thought he was going to attack you right in the courtroom."

I thanked her, hugged her, and assured her I would be careful. I still remember her kindness twenty-five years later as I walked down the remaining courthouse steps.

I knew I would have to watch my back, but I would not live in fear. I would live with caution but not fear. There is a difference. Jack would no longer keep control of any part of me, not my body, heart, mind, or soul. That was a decision I would never regret, and the best decision I ever made in that relationship.

Chapter 7

What's Next?

The only one who can truly satisfy the heart is the one who made it.

—Lois Evans

Six years later on August 13, 1999, at about one in the morning, the phone by my bed rang. I rolled over to answer it. Jack's brother informed me that Jack had been killed in a car accident, a head-on collision. A pickup truck headed in the opposite direction had tried to pass a car and wasn't able to get back into his own lane before hitting Jack's car. He was killed instantly, as was the pickup driver.

There was a flood of mixed emotions and a release of…I'm not sure how to explain all the feelings and thoughts jumbling up my head and my heart while I held the phone and listened. It was like a volcano rumbling under pressure near the surface, and then it erupted as I placed the receiver down. The dark and quiet room forced me to process not just this one moment in time, but the escape from Jack and that chapter in my life, and then everything that happened during the past six years between his arrest, imprisonment, and now death.

Jack's death felt like yet another opportunity to begin fresh in some areas of life that still needed my focus. This was the first time in nineteen years I would not have to look over my shoulder for him or think about where he was and what he was doing. I was free.

During the past six years, I worked hard to build a better life, but that didn't always mean life was easier. It was different. While I felt safer, I felt free from Jack, but it wasn't a complete freedom. With Jack's death, I felt freer to fully claim, "I have my life back. This is my life. I can really take control and not worry that anyone is going to hurt me or my children again. There's no looking back."

Although my intentions in getting out from under Jack's abusive, violent rule were good and meant to protect my family, everything didn't quite work out that way in the next few years because in hindsight there were things I could control and did well, but there were life events where I had no control.

But first, before I go more deeply into the story and emotions of these years of my life between leaving Jack and now his death, I feel a very strong need to tell you, I never ever regretted the escape! Leaving the day-to-day abuse was the hardest and scariest but absolutely the best decision I ever made. I have no doubt leaving Jack was *the* choice that kept us alive. I know as God is my witness that I wouldn't be alive today if we hadn't gotten help and gotten out.

Therefore, as I share my life, fill in the blanks of all that occurred during this time, I want you to know it is hard for me to be so transparent, so vulnerable. I wonder if I'm opening myself up to judgement and ridicule from those who do not understand; however, that is a risk I'm willing to take to reach those who need to read this story and know they are not alone.

With mixed emotions, I tell this part of my story with the hope it will help save your life or the life of someone near and dear to you. As you read the rest of this chapter, I pray if any of these thoughts or questions ring true in your own life, or you've heard another victim talk this way, you will get help. I pray in reading these pages, you will know you are not alone. I hope you will find encouragement to get help and get out too.

Please remember: Staying in an abusive relationship is never an option, no matter how hard starting over is. There is nothing better than feeling free and being alive.

You have to be alive in order to live the next chapter of your life, which may not always be easy but will be worth it. I know you too can experience more than you may have ever thought possible or felt worthy of, but you can do it if you get to safety first. Please, trust me when I tell you that everything you need to survive and thrive is within you.

In order to provide complete transparency and encouragement, I want to share some moments and emotions of that transition period with you.

While it was brave to finally take a stand and make the decision to leave Jack and try to gain control of my life again, the problem came in the fact that I didn't slow down, take a few deep breaths, and try to figure out how I ended up in such a dangerous domestic violence situation in the first place.

There's an old saying about those who don't know history, they are condemned to repeat it. I should have spent some time focusing on my history, thinking about where I came from in order to figure out what good things and bad things I took from the past and those experiences. I know now I should have reflected and gained a better understanding of my own and my family's history and legacies in order to make conscious decisions about what I wanted to carry forward and what I wanted and needed to discard.

Because I didn't stop to reflect on how I got to where I was, I kept putting one foot in front of the other in survival mode. I was so busy trying to take care of everyone else, I didn't stop to give myself some grace, some tender loving care, too.

It took a few more hard life lessons before I learned that my happiness, confidence, and worthiness could never be found in any other man or other person.

I eventually did learn: What someone else thinks of me or how they treat me was not the definition of who I am or what I will become. I am in control of allowing that treatment to occur or not. I hold the power in my own hands as to how I live my life and who I let be a part of it.

I was completely broken down emotionally, physically, spiritually during the thirteen years I was abused by Jack that I had no idea who I really was or what I was capable of. And how could I ever figure out who I really was or what I could do with my life when what Jack told me I was, was not what I believed God created me to be. I never understood how the invisible wounds inside me would affect my entire life for years to come. I didn't know to take the time to care for myself in this way.

Yes, the knife cuts had healed and scars left behind were less visible. For the longest time, the outside wounds were simply daily reminders of how close I came to dying. But now I also know those same scars are a reminder: I am a survivor. I am stronger than I gave myself credit for. I am worthy. I am capable.

But before these light bulbs of self-affirmation turned on, I found out there were invisible wounds on the inside which did not get the time and attention needed to heal. These invisible wounds to my heart and mind continued to cause self-inflicted damage.

I did indeed take control of my life, but I was not capable of letting anyone into my life totally any longer. The walls were up. No one would ever have all of me ever again. I lived on the defense for years. I might have just given up at some point and quit trying. I was generally tired, and most of all I was tired of fighting. But somehow deep down, I knew there was something to keep fighting for. If nothing else, I would keep fighting for my children. I was determined we would have the family I always dreamed of for them.

Funny, in a tragic sort of way, I see now how when looking back on these years, I never fought for me. I didn't think I deserved better than what Jack gave me. But I believed my kids did deserve so much more. It took a lot of time to heal my thoughts and expectations in order to truly move forward in my life in a healthy and meaningful way until realizing I was worthy of more for myself.

Also, with Jack, I felt I had no control, but then I tried to take too much control of my life to a point that wasn't healthy either. I had created a life where there were very few people I trusted and very few I let in.

There is a very fine line between too little and too much control, but I still wasn't sure where that line was.

As a domestic violence victim, I shut people out of my life to protect myself and the people I loved. No one was allowed to get too close to me, because they may discover the abuse and make it worse or get hurt themselves. The other part of the equation was no one could get too close or they might see my pain. They might see the damaged person I was, the damaged person I had become. I'm not sure I could have lived through having other people see me as worthless and shameful as Jack said I was. It was bad enough for my husband Jack to see me that way, it would have killed me if other people confirmed his view of me because then I'd be forced to believe he was right—and I knew he wasn't.

Somehow deep down inside me, I knew God wouldn't have created me to be seen through the eyes of people like Jack. This was my saving truth that kept getting beat down below the surface. It was going to take a whole different kind of healing for me to become whole again. That was the healing that came from faith and grace in Jesus Christ in order for my life to turn in a meaningful direction.

During the years after my escape, I ended up in two more failed relationships that I was so sure were my happily ever after—again.

I remember my sister saying to me one day, "Dawn, you're like a chameleon. Whichever man you're with at the time, you become that person. If you're dating a cowboy, you put on the starched and perfectly creased blue jeans and boots and become a cowgirl. If you're dating a doctor, you throw on your business suit and high heels and become the perfect little lady."

My sister loved me and would never have intentionally hurt me with her words. But still, these words stung. I know now it was because there was truth in what she said.

Through years of self-discovery, I thought about her words many times. I wondered why I acted this way, why I adjusted myself to please any man I chose to be with. It was years later, after I took the time to find the answer, that I figured out why.

I became different things to please different people because I had no idea who I was as a person. Since I was sixteen years old, I was always somebody's wife or mother. Having three children by the age of twenty and then becoming a grandmother at the age of thirty-four, there was never time to know or discover me and my identity.

I did the best I knew how to do surviving day by day. I became what everyone else needed me to be in the moment. That was my habit, and I was happy with living this way until it almost got me killed. I didn't even know I needed my own identity until life kept getting harder and harder to live. Everyone else was making choices for me, and I was letting them because I didn't know anything different.

I had to stop, take a few deep breaths, and look back to find out why.

Why did these things keep happening to me?

How could I keep getting everything so wrong?

Why was life not working for me?

I was trying so hard to create this idea of what a perfect world was for us. I kept a near spotless house. I cooked. I baked. I was classroom mother for each of my children. I worked a full-time job managing 125 people and did it all quite well.

Yes, I could multitask by taking care of my family and helping a neighbor or a friend.

But no matter how hard I tried, I could not get my personal life right.

I was so afraid of being hurt. I did not let anyone help me.

I was afraid if anyone knew all the ugliness in my life, they wouldn't like me. Most of the people I loved had betrayed me or left me. I truly believed I was unlovable. That who I was would never be good enough for anyone.

I eventually figured out I was *the* missing piece in this puzzle. I needed to stop focusing on everyone else and why they did "whatever." It wasn't about why they did what they did or what was broken or missing in them. I had no power or control to fix or make any of that better for them. Being their punching bag wasn't something I could fix, until I removed myself from the situation and fixed my thinking and feelings about me.

It really was about who I am.

What do I want from my life?

What drove me?

What motivated and inspired me?

What was my why?

But I couldn't really answer these questions until I did the hard work of figuring out how I got to this point in my life that it was okay for someone to hurt me so badly.

Raising three teenagers in the middle of all this starting-over was no easy task on top of everything else.

God only knows I poured all I knew how to into raising my children. I loved them the best I knew how to based on what I knew at the time. I really did my best, and no one can take that away from me or tell me otherwise. My children were fed, clothed, had a safe home to live in, and loved above all else.

But in the end, I learned that as a woman, a mother and later a grandmother, and a wife, I had control over certain things in my life and some things I had no control over at all. No matter how hard I tried, there were events and circumstances beyond my control.

These between years were hard and filled with their own set of tragedies none of us would see coming.

I started seeing signs of alcohol and drug addiction in the life of two of my children when they were still teenagers. The road of addiction in itself was filled with its own set of demons for my children. The guilt and pain I carried as a mother cannot even be put into words. The questions I asked as a mother for years afterward included:

Should I have left sooner?

What could I have done differently?

How could I have prevented this?

I could keep going down this rabbit hole over and over again, but it didn't change the here and now, which was the focus. The fact of the matter was we were alive, we were together, and we could survive anything else that came our way.

Chapter 8

Breaking Point

He heals the broken hearted and bandages their wounds.

—Psalms 147:3

The children and I had lived away from Jack for nearly five years. During this time, Jack remarried and moved to Victoria, Texas. I felt safer having him living in south Texas. The kids were older and had reestablished a relationship with Jack.

He was no longer a threat in their lives. And since they were older, I knew they could take care of themselves.

Shortly after my daughter turned sixteen years old, she came to me with the news she was pregnant. This was not that surprising to me because we had all gone down some rough roads as the teenage years unfolded. While it was not exactly the life I had imagined for my beautiful daughter, but since I was also a sixteen-year-old mother-to-be at one time, I knew we could do it as a family.

As for me at this time, I had sworn off men altogether. I knew now I would commit to help raise this little blessing. No more men to distract me!

God would just have to throw one into my lap if he wanted me married again. (Just a little spoiler: He did!)

Both of Tiffany's brothers were excited about the baby! This baby would be loved. We all got even more excited when we found out it was going to be a little boy! We all tossed names around.

I have a found memory of Tiffany and me sitting on my big king-size bed eating lemon cookies while she cried in her hormonal mess about how she would never come up with the right name. We went through nearly the entire box of lemon cookies before we had the final answer and the perfect baby name: Tristan. Then Tiffany was overcome and crying happy tears! Her baby had a name.

We were all happily anticipating Tristan's arrival in May. We made one of the bedrooms in our house into a Pooh Bear nursery. We painted. We furnished. We planned. I took control, which was what I seemed to do best. Again, I would learn I had very little control in the big picture.

Six weeks before the precious baby boy was supposed to arrive, Tiffany went into labor. Tristan was born on March 27, 1998. He weighed in at only four pounds and two ounces. But he was healthy. He was in an NICU incubator with tubes, but we could tell he was a fighter.

Tiffany loved little Tristan before he was born, and that love increased at first sight. She sat by the incubator for her turn. We rotated shifts. The doctors said he would probably have to stay in the NICU for five or six weeks. But to our surprise, ten days later, the doctors said we could take him home. The only requirement was two of us had to be trained on how to feed the formula from a special bottle designed for premature babies before leaving the hospital.

Tiffany and I both learned how to do his feedings. We set an alarm clock for every two hours. We had to wake Tristan up and feed him no matter what—every two hours. My oldest son moved back home and together we did it.

God had also dropped that special man into my lap. Nick and I had met about eight months before Tristan was born and had recently started dating. He knew the family and our circumstances. And despite our unique form of family craziness, Nick was right there with us for Tristan's weekly doctor's visits as well as helping with the every two-hour feedings around the clock. We were a team of five now.

How could anything go wrong? Tiffany stayed home with Tristan, but someone was always there to help her with his care and feeding. Everyone else worked and rotated shifts to care for Tristan.

Everyone was happy. We had fallen into a positive routine. Life was moving in a great direction for us all.

After all we had survived, I thought there was nothing left in life that could surprise me. There were no more imaginable hurtles or potholes to bring me to my knees.

Or so I thought.

I was wrong!

July 6, 1998—less than four months after Tristan was born—became a date I will never forget. It was a celebration weekend of Independence Day, July 4th.

Jack was remarried and asked Tiffany and the boys to come to the beach and bring the grandbaby. At first, the kids were just going to go for a break because it had been a long three months caring for Tristan. His doctor said he was doing great! Tristan weighed almost twelve pounds, which was right on target for a premature baby.

The doctors said there was no more need to wake Tristan up every two hours for feedings. I was hesitant for Tristan to leave. But Jack kept calling Tiffany, insisting she bring the baby. She did not want to fight with him, so she went. I knew the baby would be safe because both brothers were going to be with Tiffany and they had helped provide hands-on care and so I was not worried about that.

I was being a grandmother who was feeling protective. Even though I didn't want them to go, I knew the kids needed a break. This was how it should be. Besides, Nick and I also needed a break and some time together in our new relationship. But still, no matter how hard I tried not to worry, as they were packing to leave, I could not get rid of the feeling something bad was going to happen.

I was not worried about Jack; it had nothing to do with him. I felt very unsettled. I had those mothering instincts kicking into high gear. I couldn't help but lecture the kids to be safe and look out for each other. "Call when you arrive at Victoria." On and on I went.

Finally, Josh said, "Mom, give me Tristan. We have to get on the road. It will be fine."

I remember how I had just fed Tristan and he spit up. So I gave him a bath and changed his clothes. I hugged him and then kissed him before buckling him into the car seat. I sent the little overalls

I had bought for him to have his first pictures made in when they returned.

Two vehicles were taken because everyone could not fit into one car. It wasn't just all the baby stuff because Bryan had two friends going with him and Josh's girlfriend was riding with him in his truck. I requested that the baby ride be with Josh, he being the oldest and most experienced driver, and for a hot Texas summer, his truck had a better air-conditioner. It made me feel better. I knew they would pull over for a break whenever Tiffany needed to feed and change Tristan.

I was so relieved when I got the call they had arrived safely. During their drive, they saw an accident that had just happened and a child was thrown from the car. They got out and helped all the victims and young child until help arrived. They were shaken up but had arrived safely.

I still had a bad feeling all weekend. I thought it was just my nerves, but something in me new better.

When I get these kinds of a gut feelings, it is never wrong.

I was with Nick at his grandparent's house for the weekend. They lived on Lake Granbury. We were on Jet Skis, and I was trying to have fun and not worry. When I got back on shore, I checked my cell phone. I had missed a call from Joshua saying he was home. I was so happy they were back.

I called Josh to check on everyone and the baby. My heart about stopped when he told me Jack had talked the others into not leaving until later that night so they could spend a little more time. It was the best thing because Bryan's air-conditioner was not working well. They would leave that night to return home.

Jack had insisted the kids bring the baby down for the weekend, and then Jack stayed drunk the whole time. He spent no time with Tristan. He did not even take one picture of what would be the baby's final day. The events that happened next had nothing to do with Jack, but I still resent the time I lost with Tristan that weekend.

The kids did leave Jack's house that night to come home, but car issues made them return to their dad's house. They called me about midnight to tell they would get the car situation resolved in the morning and head home by about noontime. Jack did not answer the phone or door when they got back to his house, so Bryan boosted Tiffany into a bathroom window to get them inside.

Once inside, Tiffany fed Tristan. Bryan wanted to hold the baby and they both fell asleep on the couch. After Tiffany took a shower, she picked Tristan up and they went to bed.

The next morning, I was about to head out of the door to go to work. My heart was happy because the long weekend was over and all my kids would be home soon.

I said to myself, "I was just being silly this whole weekend. I kept myself from having fun because I worried for nothing. I have got to learn to loosen up."

I grabbed my purse and the keys when the cell phone started to ring. It was Bryan. I thought to myself, *Great! They are probably calling to tell me they are getting an earlier start and getting on the road.*

I answered the ringing phone: "Good morning, son! Are y'all about to head home?"

The phone was silent.

"Bryan, can you hear me?"

"Mom, I have to tell you something."

I froze where I was standing. I could tell by the lifelessness in his voice something was very wrong.

"Bryan, tell me!"

"Mom, Tristan is dead."

"What? No, he isn't! No, he isn't. You're wrong!"

"No, Mom, he is dead."

"No, he isn't! Why? What happened? This can't be? Where is Tiffany?"

"She is outside trying to get her baby out of the fireman's arms!"

I thought, *Her dead three-month and nine-day-old baby boy.*

I found out later Tiffany had woken up to go to the restroom and looked at Tristan. She was thinking he had slept a long time. He was asleep like he always was. One arm up over his little head. But she noticed something wasn't right. One side of his face was blue. She grabbed him and started screaming! This is how Bryan, Jack, his wife, and the rest of the house woke up that morning to a heartbroken mother's bloodcurdling screams.

Jack's wife administered CPR until the ambulance arrived. But he was already dead.

Finally, the fireman took him from Tiffany's arms wrapped him in his blanket and walked out. Tiffany ran behind the fireman, begging for her baby back. She tried to pull Tristan from his arms. They said it looked like SIDS (Sudden Infant Death Syndrome), but a full autopsy would be performed, which is standard in a child's death. We would not get our baby back for about ten days.

After receiving all the details from Bryan, I felt all life drain from me. We were never going to be okay now.

I could not fix this.

My heart was shattered. How was my little girl going to ever be okay again?

I cannot fix this hurt! I could not save her or my sons from this pain! Our life was shattered!

I called my mother and was a mess. She rushed over and picked me up off the floor. My son Joshua was not far behind. All I could do was lay on the floor sobbing, as the gut-wrenching pain of the loss tore through my body.

I could not stand up.

I couldn't function.

They loaded me into a car and drove me to a doctor and had me sedated.

I had always been so strong. I felt like I could not be broken. I was a survivor. Until now. But I didn't think I was going to survive this.

I didn't even know if I wanted to survive anymore.

This was a new level of pain I didn't know existed.

I was always solid as a rock for everyone else, but not this time. It was too much. Part of me is embarrassed to say I wasn't able to go get my son and daughter from Victoria because they had sedated me so heavily. My children were also in pain, and this was more than I could endure alone.

It was going to have to be up to someone else to step up and help pick up the shattered pieces of our lives. I had reached my breaking point.

Jack's parents made the drive and brought Bryan and Tiffany back home. I still can't believe I couldn't do it.

I still clearly remember my children arriving home that evening, carrying an empty car seat and baby swing. They left with my grandson but only came home with his belongings.

"How did this happen?"

"Why did this happen?"

There are some things in life I will never know the answer to why, and this would be one of them.

My family all came together to plan the funeral and pick out a gravesite. But we needed our baby back so we could bury him.

We were all at the funeral home when Tristan arrived. Tiffany insisted she dress him. She needed to do this, even though the funeral home advised against it because they performed an autopsy, which meant they cut the baby from the chest down and cut the top of his head off, then stitched him back together.

It didn't matter to Tiffany. She was his mother. She needed to do his final clothing.

We walked in and Tristan's cold, lifeless little body was placed in her arms. We cuddled him, talked to him, loved on him just like he was alive.

Then we clothed him.

We wrapped him in a blanket and rocked him in a rocking chair that sat next to the tiny little casket.

We could not look at him in the casket. Every day we went to the funeral home, Nick walked into the room first to get him out, then he opened the door and handed him to one of us to rock. On one of those days, I was about to enter the room to hold Tristan when my phone rang. My brother Peary was standing by my side. It was the coroner's office.

My breath sucked in, Peary grabbed the phone and said, "I'll take it for you." I nodded my head, yes. We were about to find out why our baby was lying dead in the next room. It was what they suspected, SIDS.

We would never get an answer to why.

We were told, "It just happens. It is nothing we did or didn't do. It just was."

The next day, the SIDS foundation left a book in our room at the funeral home. I will be forever grateful because that book helped us breathe again knowing what SIDS meant even though this outcome was never easy to accept.

Twenty years have passed since Tristan died, but there are still balloons, gifts, and a cake on his grave each year.

We had to figure out how to start over again and again, and again if need be. With God's help and as a family, we would find a way to stand strong in love and peace through God's grace.

Tiffany turned seventeen years old twelve days after the death of her only child. Each day, we worked hard at rebuilding what was left of our lives.

Nick and I married six months later on February 6, 1999. Nick wanted the sixth day of each month not to be a dreaded day. We agreed we would look for and find hope—together. All three of my children loved Nick. Tiffany stood beside me on our wedding day and both of my sons happily walked me down the aisle and gave their blessings to Nick.

After the wedding, we moved out of that house and into a new home we bought together. But even in the new home, Tiffany insisted we set up Tristan's nursery. We got rid of nothing. It was going to be really hard for her, for us, to let go.

I believed Tiffany would heal in her own time and in her own way. But in order to help bring healing back to her and the rest of my family, I needed to re-find my own strength and find some healing for myself.

How could I do that when I was struggling with the questions of how I became so broken and hopeless to begin with?

What was the key to my own healing?

How was I ever going to move past the abuse and pain in my life?

Could there be anything different for me? For my children?

Did I deserve more than this?

My faith told me yes, but my human heart was floundering, full of doubt.

It was becoming clearer to me that in order to fully heal myself and be strong for my family, I had to go back even further into my past, maybe all the way back to childhood, to figure out what was missing or broken in me that made me settle for less than what God intended for me.

I was still holding on tight to one tiny mustard seed of faith, but what was I going be able to do with it?

> "He replied, 'Because you have so little faith. Truly I tell you, if you have faith as small as a mustard seed, you can say to this mountain, "Move from here to there," and it will move. Nothing will be impossible for you' (Matthew 17:20).

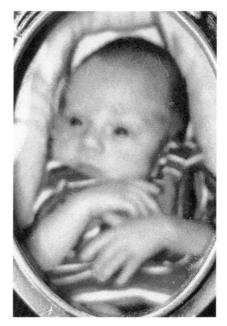

Tristan

Tiffany and Tristan

Me, Tiffany, Bryan, Joshua

Clayton and Deby Brants

Kyle, Me, Deby and Peary

My brother Hershel

Part 2

Growing Up Invisible

Me, Peary and Deby

Chapter 9

Looking for Answers

Ask and it will be given to you; seek and you will find; knock and the door will be opened to you.

—Matthew 7:7

Maybe the answers to what I needed to grow this mustard seed of faith lay in what I learned in my childhood. It was worth considering and searching. By revisiting these dark years behind me, asking and answering hard questions that might help my heart heal to a point where I could let go and truly move past all the pain, anger, unworthiness, and shame might help me and my children grow a better future. Asking and answering some tough questions might allow me and my family to move forward stronger, happier, and hope-filled. Maybe this was the key to my "happily ever after."

No matter how hard the next step would be, I knew this soul-searching work could not get done alone. And I was blessed not to have to walk this walk all alone. Even at the lowest points in my life, I knew God was always with me; he had never left me or my children.

I accepted Jesus as my Lord and Savior when I was nine years old. I was filled with the Holy Spirit when I was eleven years old. I believed in the power of his grace. I was young but confident in his place in my life. However, I was too young to fully understand then how much I'd come to rely on him for the rest of my life.

I went to church most often with my mother and grandparents. My dad and stepmother also took us to church.

One summer, Mother and Mam-Maw found a new church called Corner Stone. It was a yellow house that filled with people for one service a week on Saturday nights. It had a tent revival atmosphere where the pastor was a powerful preacher filled with the Holy Spirit.

The worship was so powerful, I could feel God's presence all over me and in the small room. I was filled with the Holy Spirit at one of those Saturday night services, and my relationship with the Lord took on a whole new meaning. Something changed within me. I knew deep in my heart and soul how powerful the name of Jesus was.

"Thank you, God, for that summer" was a prayer I've often said.

As confident as I was at such a young age about how much I needed Jesus in my life, little did I know how much I would need to lean into the power of God and his Word later on. Only God knew what lay ahead for me and the dark years to come. But even at this young age, I knew with all my heart God was good and faithful!

With God by my side through all the storms in life, I never felt totally alone.

Even when the world let me down, Jesus never does. I knew he was right there beside me, protecting me, and fighting with me. As bad as the beatings got, I knew he protected my life and the lives of my children.

While I had no way of knowing then how God would take my messy life and use it to help save other lives in the future, I did see God helping me survive one day at a time. At that time, I could ask for nothing more.

Looking back at my life, all the way back to my earliest memories, I knew without any doubt God was with me, even before I knew or accepted he was there. From the day when I was three years old and taken away from my mother, I knew God provided for me and we always walked side by side, hand in hand.

*****

Looking for answers was hard. This part of my journey could have been something that hurt relationships more. The main reason I think it didn't further damage these relationships with my family is because for me it was not about finding fault, but more about how I ended up here and why.

Another thing I realized looking back at my life, which I'd like to make clear as I write this section of the book, is in telling my story, I am not trying to blame or shame my parents or anyone else in my family. With all of that said, I am sure my parents both did the best they knew how to do at that time. They both did what they learned from their parents, who did what they learned from their parents before them. For so long, I did the same and carried on the legacies I learned throughout my life. I knew this had to change.

But this book section is about the lessons I learned, both good and bad, from each of my parents and how I discovered some insight into myself and my life to change the legacy I leave behind for future generations.

I learned how to apply the gift of forgiveness. Each of us was trying to survive the best way we could, given our circumstances. My parents and I have talked about the past and how it unfolded for each of us. Because of these conversations, we have built healthy relationships that exist to this day.

As I've grown older, I have learned to be grateful for what I've learned from each of my parents. I believe I learned the lessons I needed to get where I am in my life today.

Chapter 10

Taken Away

"For I know the plans I have for you," declares the Lord. "Plans to prosper you and not harm you, plans to give you hope and a future."
—Jeremiah 29:11

I'm not sure how much of this life-changing day, when I was three years old, I remember or how much is based on the stories I was told throughout the years.

I am, however, now very sure this is where my life took a turn that changed the way I felt and saw myself for decades to come. My lack of self-worth, tilted definition of love, and feeling invisible became ingrained in me, a part of how I saw myself and the world at this point in my life.

It was a sunny day in late October, but fall still showed up in the chill of the day.

A little red two-door Corvair driven by my father, with my new stepmother in the passenger seat, pulled into my grandparent's driveway. I remember the feeling of sadness all around. No one was smiling. Just silence.

Mother walked myself, my brother Peary who was six years old, and my sister Deby who was five years old, out the side door of our grandparent's house onto the carport. We had only one suitcase of clothes for all of us. No other personal belongings, just clothes. We never had many belongings anyway.

Peary told me Dad didn't allow him to take the two harmonicas Paw-Paw had given him.

These were Peary's only treasured possessions. He loved to play them. These instruments started a foundation for Peary's love of music that is true to this day.

When the Corvair came to a full stop, my brother and sister loaded into the back seat, and my mother placed me in my stepmother's lap in the front seat. I don't think I'd ever met this woman who my mother handed me over to. She was a small, delicate woman with dark long hair. From my perspective, I assumed by her actions she was as scared as I was at what was happening.

I still picture my twenty-nine-year-old father slamming the trunk closed after loading our one suitcase inside. Dad folded his slim but muscular, six-foot frame into the driver's seat. I remember his dark black hair kept in a short flat top like he wore when he was in the army.

He had a row of toothpicks in the liner over the driver's side window of the car. He always grabbed a toothpick to chew on before he put the car in gear.

Dad slowly backed the car out of the driveway. The passenger side window was down. My stepmother struggled to hold me down in her lap because I was leaning out of the window crying, kicking, and reaching for my mother. My screams begged her to come get me. But she just stood there with arms crossed crying quietly. I remember begging mother not to let them take me away.

We were driven from my grandparents' house, which was the only place for the first three years of my life I knew as home. My grandparents' house is to this day the one real home I ever felt like I had throughout my childhood.

I knew love here.

I knew safety here.

I knew I was not invisible here.

Mostly because of my grandparents' influence on us and my mother.

As an adult looking back at the day Dad took us away from my mother and grandparents, I have to put the story into better perspective. This was probably the single most important turning point in my life, for better and worse.

My parents divorced when I was about three months old, which led to a difficult readjustment time for my mother. I will say my dad was not abusive to my mom. Hearts were broken, and their marriage just wasn't going to survive.

Mom remarried about a year later and stayed married to this man for about a year. We thought he was a nice man and took good care of us kids. Later, Mother told us he beat her. During this marriage, we all lived together in another house within a few miles of my grandparents. When my mother and her husband divorced, we moved back into the house with my grandparents.

We lived there again for a few months when one day, my mother and grandmother got into an argument over mother staying out all night partying again. Mother did like to party, and when she partied, my grandmother was left to try and take care of the three of us while Paw-Paw worked.

Mother came and went from my grandparent's house as she pleased. Sometimes she went to work, and other times she just went out to have some fun.

Mam-Maw was too crippled with arthritis to take good care of us, even though she worked at it pretty hard.

We were young kids and needed someone who could keep up with all of us.

I remember my grandmother had all the knuckles taken out of her left foot and was left with wires hanging out of her toes until they healed. She was in a great deal of pain during this time while she tried to chase after the three of us.

The other concern for Mam-Maw and my mother was that I had already had pneumonia twice. The first time I went to the hospital with pneumonia, I was about fifteen months old. The second time, I had just turned two years old. This time, I almost died. I spent a week in the hospital under an oxygen tent. Doctors told Mother to call the family because I probably wouldn't survive through the night.

I'm not sure how I can remember the hospital room, but I do: a metal baby bed with a clear plastic tent over it. I was fighting, trying to get out, but the nurses and family kept holding me down so I could breathe in the liquid gold. I felt God's hand of grace on me. There's no other explanation for why or how I survived. God knew he had a plan for me and that night was not going to be the night my life ended.

I give credit to God for the will to live that night. Even as a small child, I learned to fight for survival, even though only God knew how much I would need to rely on this skill and instinct I was gaining this night.

My poor Mam-Maw was worried and just plain worn out! She was forty-four years old but had started dealing with the arthritis when she was twenty-four years old. She was worn out from raising seven children and now her three grandchildren. She had her first child at fifteen years old. First, a son. Then my mother and my aunt. Mam-Maw had three children by the time she was twenty years old.

I imagine the conversation between Mam-Maw and Mother before Mother decided to call my Father went something like this:

Mother said, "It's too hard to work a full-time job and then come home to take care of these three kids. I can't do it anymore."

Mam-Maw said, "I've been up all night taking care of your children. You know Dawn is either sick or never sleeps. I've got arthritis and can't do this all day and all night, every day. You need to stay home more."

Mother cried, "I don't know what else you want from me. All I know to do is call their father to come take them away from here."

This was an argument they had many times, and this time Mam-Maw didn't stop her. She called her bluff.

Mother stormed off, picked up the phone, and called my dad. She told him to come get us, she couldn't do it anymore.

I think Mother called my father partly to test my grandmother and upset her because my mother was mad at her. Mother was tired of the argument about how she needed to stop the partying and be more responsible. Mother also meant to punish my grandmother because she knew Mam-Maw didn't want us to leave.

After the phone call and plans were made with Dad, Mam-Maw begged Mother to change her mind and not send us away. Once that call to Dad was made, there was no going back.

We would not get to live with my mother again until I was nearly a teenager and I could make the decision of which parent to live with.

*****

Even though I was a little more than three years old when Mom sent us away with Dad, I still remember my grandparents' small white frame house with dark green trim around the windows and doors. There was thick, dark green St. Augustine grass growing in the front yard. I loved to walk barefoot in it because it was so soft. Maybe these memories are why St. Augustine grass is still my favorite grass to this day.

There was a huge mimosa tree in the middle of the front yard. I loved that tree with its fluffy pink flowers that smelled so sweet.

There was a big fig tree that grew next to the bedroom window in the back of the house. I have a treasured memory of Paw-Paw standing next to the tree eating a fresh fig he just picked. He held the fig in one hand and an old green water hose in the other as he filled the water cooler on those hot summer days. Paw-Paw smiled a lot and this was one of those many moments, so I could tell he was enjoying that fig.

Paw-Paw had a hard life, but still remembered to smile.

He had a daughter by a previous marriage who died of pneumonia at a few months old. I think he treated me like his own little girl because of this hole in his heart.

There were also peach trees in the very back of the yard. I'd go out and pick one right off the tree and eat it while standing right there. I never wasted time or energy to take it inside or wash it off. I stood right there in the heat of the Texas summer and let the juice run down my chin, even though the peach fuzz made my lips itch. I tried to eat as many of these peaches as possible before the worms or birds could claim them.

To this day, peaches are still my favorite fruit.

I remember the complete address and telephone number of my grandparents' little white framed house decades later. The floor plan is still vivid in my mind too, even though I left this house for the last time at seventeen years old.

Vivid memories include walking through the front door, entering into a small hall, which connected to the main hallway where an old phone bench stood holding the Yellow Pages phone book sitting on top of it. Above it in a niche was a black rotary phone.

A right turn at the end of the hallway led into the small living room. I still remember the mark a hot iron left on the old wood floor. I remember sitting on that floor, near that spot, the day I heard Elvis died.

The next room was an L-shaped kitchen with a gray and white Formica table where we had supper every evening with Mam-Maw, Paw-Paw, and Mother. There wasn't always a lot of food. Some days, supper was a pot of pinto beans we ate on for three days. Some days we also got fried potatoes and ketchup. No matter what was for dinner, Paw-Paw always wanted sliced white bread on the dinner table so he could literally clean off his plate. Every time we sat down to a meal at that table with my Paw-Paw, we knew grace was spoken over the meal before we ever touched it.

"Dear heavenly Father, we thank you for the blessing you put before us. Thank you for the food, for the nourishment of our bodies. In Jesus's name, we pray. Amen."

The carport door stood just in front of the table. There was a small white gas stove to the right of the door. The clearest memory I have of that stove was my mother and aunt lighting cigarettes off of it. They'd light the cigarettes and run out the carport door to sit in lawn chairs and watch the kids ride bikes up and down the street.

As a small child, I remember standing in front of the stove, where a big white ceramic sink set to the right, and the refrigerator was just to the right of the sink. Even as a small child, I could touch the stove and refrigerator at the same time.

I was small and so was this kitchen. It was like I fit perfectly here, in this kitchen, and in this house.

There was one very small bathroom the six of us shared to the left of the kitchen. Directly across from the bathroom was a bedroom with a window that looked into the backyard. I could see out this window to the peach trees while sitting in bed. It was in this very room I later brought my first son Joshua home from the hospital the day he was born.

There were three bedrooms total. There was one more bedroom at the end of the hall. That bedroom had a window that looked into the front yard and one window that looked into the neighbor's carport. I remember a black enamel painted four-poster bed in that room where my grandparents slept.

The whole house was only about 890 square feet. While the house was small, the place it has in my heart is huge. It always felt safe to me. I know now it wasn't the house, but the love, security, and so much more my grandparents gave me that made it home.

Little did I know at three years old, when the car left that driveway, it would be us against the world. As we were driven away in the red Corvair, an unspoken bond was formed between the three of us that neither time nor distance would break apart. And it was this bond that helped us survive the dark years which lay ahead. If we had nothing else ever again, we would always have each other.

Only the death of my sister in 2012 broke us physically apart, but she will live in our hearts as long as we live.

Even though we were blessed with two more brothers whom each of us loves, one through my mom and one through my dad, Peary, Deby, and I had an inseparable bond unlike any other.

Chapter 11

Starting a New Life

I know the Lord is always with me. I will not be shaken, for He is right beside me.
—Psalms 16:8

I was worn out from crying, screaming, and begging for my mother as the car pulled away from the people I love the most. I settled down, worn out by grief, my main focus turned to the drive itself. It seemed as if that little red Corvair would never get to where it was taking us. Three and a half hours of sadness and silence filled the car until we reached a new place we knew nothing about. What I remember most about the long drive was the pine trees popping up all around us. Decades later, I still feel sadness creep over me every time I see pine trees.

We finally pulled into a small driveway where there was a small pale green single wide trailer. Inside there were two bedrooms and one small bathroom. What I recall most about that night was feeling sick as we walked up the cement steps and through the trailer door. Compared to my grandparents' house, which was small, this was very tiny.

I know now, it was all my dad and stepmother thought they needed. She was six months pregnant with their first child at this time, and they had no idea that overnight they would take on my dad's other three children.

We only lived in the small trailer where the three kids shared a bedroom for a few months. Then dad bought a small green frame house not far away. It had three bedrooms, a living room, kitchen, and bathroom. There were four cement steps that led up to the front door and a small cement porch. By then, my new little brother Kyle was born.

Even though I was only four years older then, Kyle, Dad, and my stepmother called me his "little mother" because I always wanted to take care of him. They told me I would stand and hold Kyle's bottle through the bars of his crib.

It took him longer to talk because I always talked for him. If he wanted something, it was always me who spoke up for him or just got whatever he needed. I loved him so much and as bad as we didn't want to be there at my father's house, Kyle was a good reason to stay. At least he was some light in my darkness.

We lived with Dad for about eight years, until I was eleven years old. The hardest part of leaving, for all three of us, was leaving Kyle behind. He was Dad's son and had a different mother, so we had no real choice in the matter, but that didn't make it hurt any less. That day when we left, it was like leaving a piece of my heart behind.

*****

When I was seven years old, Dad bought a thirty-three-acre farm. It had a red brick house on it with three bedrooms, a den, a living room, a kitchen, and a big front porch. Dad converted the garage into a master bedroom for him and his wife. The girls shared a bedroom and the boys shared another bedroom.

Off the front porch, you could see two huge oak trees in the big front yard. One of these trees had a big tire swing made from a large cattle rope with a big tractor tire tied onto it. My sister and I used to sit in it together and our brothers would push us when we went out to play.

We were not allowed much time to play and have fun because there was always so much work to do on the farm. Dad owned the 33 acres we lived on, another 22 acres next to it, and 180 acres down the road for a total of 235 acres. Besides working a full-time job at the steel factory, Dad also raised cattle: Angus Herford and Brahama bulls. He had about 120 head of cattle at a time.

We had a half-acre garden with the straightest rows ever seen. This was an example of how meticulous my dad was about everything. The garden grew squash, cucumbers, snap peas, tomatoes, okra, and other vegetables for our family to eat.

Every free moment we had, Dad had us in the garden pulling the weeds or picking the caterpillar worms off the leaves of the Katanka trees that lined the fence around the garden. We picked the worms for Dad to sell as fishing bait. Those caterpillars could bite, and the bite really hurt.

I have very few good memories from the time we arrived on that chilly fall night in 1964 at the small trailer steps until the day we left the farm in the summer of 1971.

The one thing we had to look forward to during these years were the summers when we went back to live with my mother wherever she was living at the time. It was like being let out of prison and leaving the fear, intimidation, and control behind. We could breathe again, smile, get a hug, and play. I didn't feel surrounded by fear or dread on those summer days.

When I was on the farm, I would go to sleep every night by saying to myself, "I am not afraid because Jesus is with me." I'd say this over and over until sleep would finely come. In the summertime, I felt God all over me all the time.

Chapter 12

Lessons Learned from Dad and His Family

That which does not kill us makes us stronger.
—Friedrich Nietzsche

From the first night when we arrived at that small green trailer, our lives were filled with rigid rules and great fear about punishment. My dad believed in strict discipline. He was only going to say something once. After that, there were severe consequences.

He believed kids talked only when spoken to. He lived the old philosophy of children should be seen and not heard. He didn't care and didn't have the time to care about what we were thinking or how we felt.

He taught us impeccable manners though: Yes, sir. No, sir. Please. Thank you.

These were all the words he wanted to hear from us.

There was no asking, "Why?" The answer was always "Because I said so."

We learned to do what we were told without question. This is when I feel I began to lose my voice. At this young age, I was learning to become invisible. Living invisible meant safety.

There was no explanation, no discussion, just follow orders.

Anytime we went somewhere, we looked like baby ducks all lined up in a row. We had to walk single file in the grocery store or anywhere else we went in public. Like his garden planted in impeccable rows, we traveled in a similar impeccable formation. This is another example of how Dad believed in perfection.

He didn't believe in praise. There were always things that needed to get done and everyone had assigned duties.

I felt like no matter how hard I tried, I could never measure up to his standards of perfection. Nothing I did was good enough. The attention I got from my dad was negative and punishing.

Our days were planned out for us from the time we woke up until we went to bed. Even on the coldest mornings, we were not allowed to sleep in or enjoy the warmth of our beds. The minute our eyes opened and the feet hit the ground, we had to make our beds before we did anything else. My sister made her half of the bed and I made mine. We had to lay out our clothes the night before so we wasted no time getting dressed.

Breakfast was almost always lumpy oatmeal that made me throw up. I'd get in trouble and get a spanking for throwing up the oatmeal.

I was forced to go back to the table, gag, and swallow the rest of that meal.

After a few months of this vicious routine, I was allowed to eat cold cereal instead.

We fed the cats, dogs, and whatever other animals were hanging around the house every morning before my stepmother took us to school.

We treasured the recess time at school the most.

Every few months, one of us would get brave enough to ask my stepmother for some money to buy candy. Every time we asked, she gave us each some money. We earned an allowance for doing our chores, but we couldn't use it. We each had our own banks in our rooms where were told to save our money. I'm still not sure why or what we were saving for.

I'm sure my dad was trying to teach us to be responsible with our money and save it for something big or special, but he never explained his thought process to us. I remember asking once to use some of my money to buy hair spray. His response was, "I don't know if you're old enough to be using hair spray. You better go ask your momma."

After asking her, she did take me to buy some hair spray with my own money.

The boys used some of their money to buy a calf.

I wonder sometimes if dad would have let us do more or have more if we had asked. But the truth of the matter is that he made us too afraid to ask for much or anything.

After years of this silent torment, all of us had lost our voices. We learned to live most of our life invisible.

At the end of the school day, we'd often ask our stepmother if we could walk home on pretty days. We lived about two miles from school. We loved to walk because we knew when we got home there were hours of chores waiting. On the walk, we'd stop to pick blackberries. We ate a lot of the berries on the way home, but when some berries did make it home, my stepmother either made a pie or served them in a bowl with milk and sugar. These were the good memories.

Every Saturday was housecleaning and chore day. We each had our assigned chores. When Dad came home, he inspected our work. If it didn't meet his standard, we were spanked and had to do it all again. Not just the area that was missed or didn't meet his expectations, but all of the dusting, for instance.

Spankings and fear were the normal operations and feelings around Dad's house.

Since I wasn't the smartest of the four, the prettiest, the skinniest, the most athletic, the most anything, I never measured up. I mostly went unnoticed, becoming more invisible.

It was during this time with Dad that I began to feel invisible. I tried my best to perform well for Dad, but it was never enough. Nothing I did was ever good enough.

Even though I was a straight A student through fifth grade, my sister and brother always received recognition for being smarter. School was always harder for me than it was for them.

There was a time when I was a little chunkier than Deby, so Dad would take the potatoes or bread from my plate and give them to Deby, who didn't want the extra food but was forced to eat it anyway. We were not allowed to leave the table until we ate everything on our plate.

Dad had a thick leather belt he wasn't afraid to use. It left bruises on our butts and legs that took weeks to heal.

I remember when we came home from school, we were only allowed to have one piece of hard candy to eat. No other snacks. One day we were so hungry after school, the four of us decided to sneak one little pack of peanuts out of the big sack Dad kept for his lunches. The four of us split the little three- or four-ounce sack of peanuts while my dad and stepmother were still at work. Those peanuts were delicious.

A few days later, Dad realized a pack of his peanuts was missing and told us all to line up in the kitchen. He gripped his big leather belt tightly. We were scared to death.

His voice became deeper and sterner. He would raise his eyebrow and glare at us, "Someone better tell me who ate my peanuts. Or I'll line you all up and give you each licks with this belt."

My oldest brother Peary stepped forward. He wasn't going to let us all get hit. He told Dad he took the peanuts. I thought dad was never going to quit hitting him with that belt.

The bruises left on Peary's legs, back, and butt made me sick. And the memory of watching Peary getting whipped still sickens me to this day as I sit here writing about it.

I also hated nighttime. Dad walked in the hall between the bedrooms and popped the leather belt. "You'd better keep it quiet and get to sleep," he threatened.

Fear became my constant companion from a young age.

Living with my Dad was hard. While Dad went to work every day to provide a roof over our heads and put food on our plates, he never provided any emotional connection. While the dinner table had plenty of food, there was no conversation or even the slightest interest about how our day went, how we felt, or what we needed or wanted. He didn't know who we were or what made us happy, and he didn't have time for such nonsense.

What was missing was love, nourishment, positive words of encouragement, hugs, and laughter.

What the time with him lacked was human, heartfelt connection.

Looking back, I know this time of my life made me feel invisible for many reasons. If I was invisible at home, maybe I wouldn't get spanked. If I stayed invisible at school, maybe I wouldn't get in trouble for talking out loud and get sent home to be spanked. I was invisible because we weren't allowed to connect much with other people. We didn't have time for friendships, so I hid from most friendship connections too.

I always wanted Dad to love me. I wanted his hugs and positive affirmation, but I knew he wasn't going to love me like he did Deby. She was his obvious favorite. But even with that being said, he didn't love her like a little girl longing for her father to love her. She never received much positive attention from him either.

Deby always wished Dad would tell her she was pretty. So did I. But it wasn't going to happen. He just wasn't capable for whatever reason; it really didn't matter. Or maybe he just didn't know he was supposed to love us in this way.

I eventually came to the point where it wasn't worth trying to earn Dad's love and attention any more. I'm not sure Deby ever stopped trying to earn Dad's love. It was safer and easier for me to stay invisible than to keep getting hurt. I wish Dad would have told us about his childhood when we were young; maybe I would have understood him more.

As I grew older, I learned my dad never received love from his parents either. My dad was the oldest of two boys. At twelve years old, my father was driving tractors and combines to earn his own money. His father was an alcoholic who stole my father's hard-earned money to drink and gamble. My grandfather was also abusive to Dad's mother.

I remember when I was about eight years old, going to visit my grandmother one time when she had a broken arm. I was told she slipped on a wet floor. I wondered how true this was knowing that my grandfather was an abusive drunk. Years later, I asked my dad about this and he did confirm my suspicions that his father had caused her the broken arm.

We didn't visit Dad's family very often, and I felt there were hidden secrets no one wanted to talk about. As a grown woman, I learned that the silence was all attributed to the abuse and drinking. But one of my favorite memories of visiting my grandmother, Ma Wood, was her tea cakes. The raw dough was delicious by itself. It was a delicate, thin, airy, cake-like cookie with the slightest hint of vanilla flavor.

My father told me a story once about how he would send money home to his mother for several years. She would put it in tin cans and bury it in the barn. My father found out later that his father had stolen all the money to gamble and drink with.

Therefore, while my dad didn't love me the way I wanted and needed to be loved as his little girl, I think it was because he didn't know what real love from a parent was or how to give it either.

As I grew older, I learned more and more about this legacy of silence that also impacted my father.

The other thing I think that is worth mentioning is five decades ago the role of the men, husbands, and fathers in a family was very different than it is today. Men were considered good husbands and fathers if they had a job and earned enough to pay for housing, food, and the basics.

What I learned from my dad was a strong work ethic, good manners, and a sense of responsibility. He taught me to be resilient. While these were tough lessons I learned as a child, they helped me survive the violent storms that lay ahead as an adult.

Some of the negative lessons I learned as a child growing up which I didn't recognize were damaging parts of my family legacy were:

Silence was protection.

Punishments were to be expected when I didn't meet expectations.

Fear and control by men were a normal, expected part of life.

And I didn't like feeling invisible and unloved. I hoped that someday someone would see me and love me for who I was.

*****

Our dad and stepmother would take us to church. Not every Sunday, but often. They did believe in the Lord and did their best to make sure we had a Christian foundation as well.

It was a foundation I trusted and believed in because I noticed that when I was in church, I didn't feel scared. Instead, it was a time for me to breathe and hear a message of hope.

One Sunday, as the preacher ended the service with a call for salvation, I felt something in my heart I had never felt before. My sister must have felt the same thing because we looked at each other, grabbed hands, and walked down the church aisle together: two lost, lonely little girls who had found hope in the one thing we could not see, feel, or touch. But somehow we each knew we would never be alone again.

Christ was living in me. I felt true hope for the first time in my young life.

"Maybe, just maybe, we were going to be okay." It was a hope, a prayer, a question, and a deep desire.

It wasn't just the three us of us anymore. Now we had God no matter where we were. From that moment on, I knew no matter how scared I was, I had someone on my side fighting for me. Little did I know then the fight that lay ahead of me as the years passed by; I would call upon my new friend and heavenly Father many more times in the dark years ahead.

Chapter 13

Lessons Learned from Mom and Her Family

So do not fear, for I am your God. I will strengthen you and help you; I will uphold you with my righteous right hand.

—Isaiah 41:10

Looking back, it was interesting to see how life repeats itself, how legacies are born and keep playing out until someone noticed the direction and stops or changes the legacy.

For example, my grandmother had three children by the time she was twenty years old, and her first child was born when she was fifteen years old. My mother also had three children by twenty years old and was pregnant with her first child when she was sixteen years old. And I myself repeated the cycle with three children born by the time I was twenty years old, and pregnant with the first one when I was also sixteen years old. My daughter had her first child when she was sixteen years old as well. The women in our family were strong, I will say that. When life got tough, it made us get tougher.

But later in life, as I tried to figure out what led me to where I was, where I thought being abused was a part of love, I learned there were other family legacies that had been passed down.

My mother's father was very abusive to my grandmother and to the children. He repeatedly beat her and them. My grandmother was the first person I knew who was a domestic violence victim. Her first husband was abusive, but then she married my Paw-Paw who would teach us all what real love looked like. My mother married my father who never hit her, but she did eventually follow in the footsteps of domestic violence with other men. Then I repeated the pattern when I married Jack.

My mother's father left the family when she was only five years old. He just seemed to disappear, never to be seen again.

Just like that, he vanished!

People always thought my grandmother's brother had "done something" to him because of his "disappearance." However, about fifty years after he left, by a very weird circumstance, the family found out he died alone, on the streets, as a homeless old man.

He was also a physically abusive and violent alcoholic, not just to his wife but to others. For instance, he threw my uncle down some stairs, causing him to break his arm.

But God blessed my grandmother, because after her first husband disappeared, she met the man I knew and loved as my grandfather. With him came four boys, so now my grandmother was the mother to seven children total: three of hers (including my mother) and four of his.

*****

We lived with Dad during the school year and spent summers with Mom at either our grandparents' house or in Mom's house if she was married. Mother married several different men by the time she was forty-nine years old. She sometimes happened to marry men with money, so sometimes we had money too.

The love of her life was her last husband. He died of cancer after they were married about two years. Mom was an alcoholic up to this point, but the grief caused her to quit drinking and she found her faith in God.

My mother was always very pretty and likable. She loved a good party above all else.

She was a free spirit and liked to try fun and unusual things. One time, my mother and her sister performed as a trapeze act with the circus in town when Mom was about six years old. Their career ended when her sister didn't catch my mother who fell to the ground and broke her arm. We all shake our heads and still laugh about this story at all our family events to this day.

Although there were many happy times for my mother growing up, there wasn't much food to eat, or much of anything else that might today be considered normal, like sheets on the bed and a curtain on the bedroom window. They were poor. To survive, my mother would steel onions and potatoes from the neighbors' garden of the things left behind after their harvest. It was food the neighbor didn't want, but her family didn't have the ability to be that picky.

As a little girl, my mother went into the hospital often. She would break out in hives from nerves and stress that made her skin crack and bleed. The treatments required bandages on her feet, legs, arms, and hands to heal. But it was not all bad news, because it meant there would be sweet nurses to love on her and give her attention. She had her own bed to sleep in with clean sheets. And enough food for her belly to be full.

Later on, the times we lived with my grandparents were challenging in some ways, but full of love and nurturing that made everything else seem all right.

Mom started working as a bartender at local bars at a young age. The job suited her since she was very social, loved to party, and then became a heavy drinker. She did not like responsibility.

I thought Mother was the prettiest woman I had ever seen. She had beautiful blonde hair and would wear a long blonde fake ponytail on the tip of her head. She had a great figure. I remember thinking how much she looked like the actress in the *I Dream of Jeannie* television program.

Men also thought mother was beautiful!

As I got older, I realized most of the men she dated or married had shady and violent pasts. Thank goodness, my dad was the only exception.

Mother grew up poor. She dropped out of high school in the tenth grade because she was pregnant with my brother. She had no job skills. She was married to my father at this time, and they lived in the nearby army post. About thirteen months after my brother was born, my mother gave birth to my sister, and then fifteen months after that, she gave birth to me. We were a family of five living paycheck to paycheck, and times were tough. Mother stayed home to take care of the three children because it really didn't make sense for her to pay someone else to come in to take care of us.

Three months after I was born, my mother and father divorced. Mother and the three of us went to live with my grandparents.

There was never any doubt that Mam-Maw and Paw-Paw loved us. And they loved each other.

*****

From as far back as I can remember, Paw-Paw drove the bus for a church in downtown Fort Worth. When we lived with mom during the summers, I would ride the church bus with Paw-Paw every Sunday morning. He was in the driver's seat, and I sat right behind him. We stopped at house after house around town to pick up families or people who didn't have their own cars or other means of transportation to get to church. I remember how Paw-Paw put his large winkled hand on the big metal handle that swung around to open the big bus doors.

Paw-Paw always smiled and greeted each person who walked up those church bus steps. I smiled and greeted everyone who passed my way too. It was times like these I felt like I belonged, I mattered.

Paw-Paw and I always walked into church together. We sat together listening to the preacher. I'd sit still and tried hard to focus on the message when a faint snoring sound broke through to catch my attention. I would look up and sure enough Paw-Paw's head was toppled over to one side. He was sound asleep and snoring.

The memory of our Sunday routine still makes me smile all these years later. I was happy with my Paw-Paw. He represented love, safety, and consistency to me.

I was in a class one time when I was asked to think back to the first person I remember feeling loved by. I thought for a few minutes and without a doubt it was my grandparents.

They always made time for me and made me feel special.

Paw-Paw died when I was fourteen years old.

As brokenhearted as I was on that day, I am thankful to this day he did not live to see the pain my adult years held. I know it would have broken his heart in two.

Mam-Maw died the day after my thirtieth birthday. She was an amazingly courageous woman. For example, she taught herself to drive when she was more than fifty years old because Paw-Paw had gotten sick with emphysema and couldn't drive anymore. He couldn't work anymore either. And as crippled as she was with her rheumatoid arthritis, she went out and got a job at a corner 7-Eleven convenience store where she stood on her feet for nine hours a day. She earned the money to pay all the bills since Paw-Paw wasn't able to anymore.

I didn't realize then how hard she worked or how many hours Mam-Maw stood on her poor little feet to buy me a dress for the ninth grade sports banquet. A family friend who played football invited me to go with him to the end-of-school-year celebration.

The floor-length green chiffon dress that flowed when I walked cost ninety dollars, which was a lot of money more than forty years ago. Imagine only making about three dollars per hour. That was almost a week's worth of pay, after taxes and things, to buy me this dress.

But I felt beautiful in that dress! I still remember it clearly. For the first time in my life, I felt beautiful and raised my head high with confidence as my green chiffon dress flowed out behind me with each step I took as the doors to the banquet hall opened. I belonged here with the other beautiful teenage girls. I was not invisible on this night. Thank goodness my mother taught me how to feel like I belonged.

The feeling of belonging was important to her because she said she always felt out of place. My mother wanted her children to feel accepted and not embarrassed to go to new places and experience new things.

Mother always believed in living good when we could. She would take us to very nice restaurants and teach us how to eat lobster and order a steak. I have eaten and worked at some five-star restaurants, and never once did I feel out of place or not know how to use the right fork because of my mother's teachings.

We may have had to eat beans for a week after one of these outings, or hope to have electricity the next month, but for Mother it was worth it.

*****

Although I learned how to love and belong from my mother, there are other legacies I learned that needed to get broken. Some of these I unknowingly took and repeated in my own life, which I now clearly know are legacies that need to stop.

Some of mother's lack of confidence and lack of money led her to pick men who were abusive. When she first met a man, he made promises and treated her well, showered her with lots of attention. Most of them charmed her and promised her the happily ever after she always longed for. She was always looking for someone to love her.

My mother's generation was taught to get married and that they needed a man to survive. Most women who went to college went to find a husband.

What I saw from my mother also taught me that when you're a parent, life could not always be a big, nonstop party. And while it sounds good to live life to the fullest, there are times when it is important to accept responsibility.

With few rules to follow and little supervision, children can get in trouble. Children need a balance of discipline and love to help them feel secure. Unfortunately, it would take most of my adult life before I truly knew how important these lessons were for raising the next generation.

Chapter 14

Childhood Memories

When we forgive evil we do not excuse it, we do not tolerate it, we do not smother it. We look the evil full in the face, call it what it is, let its horror shock and stun and enrage us, and only then do we forgive it.

—Lewis B. Smedes

Summers were always the best! We couldn't wait until the last day of school to head back to Fort Worth. Summers meant fun. Sleeping in. Laughing. Silliness. And one of the most exciting ends to our summers was the joint birthday party for all of the children.

My little brother Hershel's birthday was actually August 13th. But since Mom did not get to be with us on our birthdays because we were with Dad, she made it a special celebration that included us all.

At Dad's, we each got a birthday pie with two dollars under our plate as our gift. Not much excitement or celebration.

But in the summers, on my brother's birthday, Mother threw a party for all four of us. The boys got their own birthday cake and my sister and I got our own birthday cake. The girl's cake was always so beautiful. It was always a white cake with white frosting and little ballerinas dancing on top.

The party always took place under the carport of my grandparents' house. It was my favorite spot in the world. All the neighborhood kids were able to come spend time with us. We all ate cake and ice cream. Then we played games.

Because of these memories, I love beautiful birthday cakes. As a parent, I made sure my kids had one every year. These memories make me feel happiness and love.

Other hot summer days were filled with Sunday church, then Paw-Paw would get a big watermelon and ice it down.

Mother, my aunt, and our families including Mam-Maw and Paw-Paw would go to Lake Worth and swim. Then we'd sit on the beach and eat ice-cold watermelon.

There were two very memorable events that happened while at that beach.

One was with my sister and I holding hands jumping up and down in the water when all the sudden, I fell into a drop-off. I remember dropping under that dark murky water several times. My toes would hit the ground and I would try to bounce back up, but I was too short. I just kept going under, over and over again sinking into the darkness where I couldn't breathe.

I tried to grab a lady standing there, but she just stared at me. Frozen. Unable or unwilling to help.

I was filled with panic. Choking on water and overcome with fear in the darkness, I wasn't going to stop trying, stop fighting, but fear and water were filling my lungs.

The next thing I knew, I could see light.

I could breathe again.

All at once, someone had jerked me up out of the water. I could breathe fresh air again.

I was safe.

Safe in the arms of my Paw-Paw. He sacrificed his Sunday's best church suit, his wallet, and anything else he was carrying at the time to save me. We didn't always have very much, but we knew we always had each other to love.

There he was holding me tightly. He had seen me struggling. As soon as he saw me going under, he didn't hesitate a bit. He jumped in, suit, wallet, and all.

I was not invisible to Paw-Paw. I knew he loved me.

I can still remember Paw-Paw's wallet and its contents spread out on the carport table to dry.

The next incident and childhood memory was really kind of funny.

My aunt took us to the beach one day and Mother was going to meet up with us later on. So my sister, cousin, and I were playing on the beach while my aunt lay on a blanket tanning.

When my mother arrived, she saw the other kids but could not find me. In a panic, she asked my aunt where I was. My aunt said I had been right there, but then I disappeared. No one could find me. Every kid on the beach was called out of the water. All the grownups were wading through the water trying to find me. All were moving their legs slowly in case I was at the bottom.

Security was called. Everyone was crying and panicked.

Mother said the next thing she knew, I came walking down the beach. Everyone came running up to me. I had no idea what was going on.

Everyone was asking, "Where were you?"

"In the bathroom."

I'm not sure if they wanted to hug me or spank me, but they ended up settling on happiness. I was found, even though I never really felt like I was lost. I got lots of hugs!

I had not told anyone I was going to the restroom, which was up at the top of the hill. It was made out of cement, so I never heard anyone calling me.

I felt loved.

On other hot summer nights, mother spread a big white sheet under the mimosa tree in the front yard and the neighborhood kids would come over. Mom would tell us ghost stories or funny stories.

If we got bored, we had a scavenger hunt. All the neighbors participated. We mostly put things on the list we wanted to eat, like a slice of pickle with seasoning salt on it.

How I loved those summer nights.

But then like all good things, it came to an end.

School was about to start, so back to the farm we went where life was full of rules, fear, and hard work.

When I was about fourteen years old, back living with Mother full-time during the school year, she and us kids were living with her then-boyfriend. He was good to Mother and us kids. Mother's hair was always done nicely. She had beautiful black car and nice clothes. She seemed happy.

Then one day, they got into an argument while we were gone somewhere. The next day, we all moved back in with my grandparents.

When I came home from school the next day, mother was sitting in a lawn chair under the carport and was crying. Panicked, I ran to her and asked what was wrong. She looked up with haunted eyes and said her boyfriend was killed that morning while taking out the trash. Someone hid in the bushes and shot him with a rifle. It turned out there was an organized, paid-for hit on him. He was a mobster.

They waited to do the hit on him until we were moved out. I guess there is some sort of a code of ethics between mobsters, believe it or not.

There was a great sadness in Mother's eyes after that.

This was our life. Mother had numerous relationships and marriages throughout our growing-up years.

Another relationship Mother was in which haunts me to this day was with a man when I was about sixteen years old and pregnant with my first son.

I was married and lived in a duplex just a few streets over from where mother was living with this new man.

Late one evening, my telephone rang and Mother told me to meet her at the hospital.

This man had come home in a jealous rage over something and beat Mother nearly to death. He kicked out her front tooth and then took a sheet and hung her up to an electric fixture. He left her alone there to die.

She was able to somehow fight her way out of the noose.

When I arrived at the hospital, she looked like a terrified, wounded animal.

Her tooth was kicked out and bruises were forming all around her face and neck.

That is still a hard event for me to let go of and forgive to this day. But I have forgiven, because God is all about the power of forgiveness, and no one can move forward in life and become all God has created them to be until learning forgiveness.

Forgiveness. It is a powerful weapon and tool.

When bitterness resides in your heart, it is a weapon Satan can use it against you to create strife and hatred in life. Life's full potential will never come to pass without applying the tool of forgiveness.

I don't think Mother ever truly found happiness until 1981, when she met a man named Jerry. He was fun-loving and accepted Mother for exactly who she was. They were happy. Then after a few years of marriage, he was diagnosed with cancer. Mother took care of him until his death.

Then she gave herself to the Lord and at forty-nine years old, she quit drinking, partying, and smoking cigarettes.

The only people she wanted to love after that were the Lord and her family.

For the years that led up to this point, mother had suffered and lost much at the hands of many men.

One thing about Mother, she always believed in the Lord even though it took years for her to start believing she was all God said she was.

The next pivotal moment in my life that would lead me to a greater understanding of God's love for me was the summer when I turned eleven. That summer, when we went to visit Mother, we stayed to live with her. It was the summer we told our parents we were never going back to the farm.

We were old enough to decide not to go back to the farm. At least my brother and sister were, and in six months I would be too. A court fight could last that long. So the three of us made a stand, no longer allowing ourselves to be invisible. And as always, the three of us stood together and said, "No more."

Chapter 15

Real Truths

Surely God is my salvation; I will trust and not be afraid. The Lord, the Lord himself, is my strength and my defense; he has become my salvation.

—Isaiah 12:2

There were many things I learned about myself and my life by taking the time after the escape and in the years that followed to pray, reflect, and heal. By looking back at my childhood and young adulthood, I did learn lessons from my parents, which were both positive and negative, but all of which shaped me in some way.

I know this.

I accept this.

And in many ways, I am grateful for this journey, because it is what makes me who I am today. This path has opened up doors for me to show God's love and speak his truths into the lives of other domestic violence victims in the hopes they will see that escape and healing are possible for them too.

As a child of God, here are a few examples of the real truths I carry with me to this day.

First, control is not love and love is not control. These two words and feelings are not interchangeable treatments by a loved one.

When someone needs to know your every move, gives you a time to be home or else, and accuses you of things they are probably doing themselves, it is all a mind game! When someone claims to love you and works overtime to separate you from others who love you, like family, that is not love. Love is not violent. Love should not leave physical or emotional cuts and bruises.

Feeling loved is feeling accepted for who you are, as you are.

Love is an "as is, where is" deal.

In an abusive situation, love is not the driving force because it is about the abuser's needs and wants to control all the time.

A loving relationship is when each party is willing and able to give 100 percent of themselves for the good of both people.

Love does not hurt like this. It does not hit, it does not smother, it does not control.

What love really is can be found in 1 Corinthians 13:4: "Love is patient. Love is kind. It does not envy, it does not boast, it is not proud."

Second, when I first met Jack, he made me feel wanted, loveable, and invincible, but what I learned is that true love, true invincibility, came from my relationship with Jesus Christ, not through any man or other human being. There is no love or invincibility that matters like that found in the promises in God's Word and his promises. The belief that God created each of us for a special purpose and that each of us matters to God is where our real internal strength comes from. It is the only strength that lasts and never fails.

I know this to be true because God led me to my life verse. It guides everything I do both personally and professionally: "For I know the plans I have for you," declares the Lord, "Plans to prosper you and not to harm you. plans to give you hope and a future" (Jeremiah 29:11).

Third, being a young woman, I always thought it was my responsibility to fix things. I'd tell myself, "If I can change this one thing, it will change Jack's behavior." "If I made more money, he'd stop hitting me." "When his baby is born, he'll quit the drugs." I made excuses and did this with Jack over and over and over and over and over again. But the real truth is I had no control over what Jack did or didn't do. For whatever reason, he didn't fight his demons and I wasn't responsible for fighting them for him. I couldn't control him or his actions. His behavior wasn't in any way my fault. Any change in him had to come from inside himself. We can only control our own hearts, our own paths. To believe we can do more is stepping into God's shoes. No human is able to fill those shoes, but we can walk in his footsteps and make the choice to follow his Holy Spirit who directs our paths.

> "But the fruit of the Spirit is love, joy, peace, forbearance, kindness, goodness, faithfulness, gentleness and self-control. Against such things there is no law" (Galatians 5:22–2).

Finally, there is the issue of family legacy. Looking back on my life, I realize a very dangerous legacy was being passed down from generation to generation: the legacy of domestic violence. My grandmother, mother, myself, and now my daughter, had become victims of domestic violence. It wasn't until my daughter followed this pattern that I knew I had to break my silence once again in order to change the legacy I left behind for my grandchildren and future generations to come.

It is the concern for this legacy with my children, and the children of others in similar situations, which has led me to become a victim's advocate and commit my life to redirecting and rebuilding family legacies.

To think the children who grow up in homes with domestic violence don't know what is happening is hiding them from the truth. The best parent thinks we are protecting our children from hearing or seeing the violence, but we are not and cannot. The innocents hear more and see more than you may ever know. I know this to be true from personal experience and from stories I hear from other survivors.

We have to protect our children, God's children, and break the legacy of domestic violence and the silence that surrounds it. "He heals the brokenhearted and binds up their wounds" (Psalms 147:3).

The truths mentioned in this chapter only scratch the surface of my faith in God and belief in his promises for me, and for all of his children. In the next section of this book, I will go into more depth of my understanding and the application of God's Word in my life.

Chapter 16

Life on My Own

"He says," Be still, and know that I am God;
I will be exalted among the nations, I will be
exalted in the earth."
—Psalms 46:10

It's kind of funny, really, how life can take such a U-turn. I was nineteen years old with a twenty-two-month-old son and a ten-day-old newborn son—and right smack in the middle of a divorce. I was working so hard trying to create what I thought was the perfect happy little family.

My mother was kind enough to let me live with her the last couple months of my pregnancy, when my old bartending boss decided I shouldn't work any longer. But now I was getting kicked out of her apartment because she was about to get remarried.

I was moving my children and myself into a one-bedroom apartment where my grandmother already lived. I slept on the couch with Josh by my side, and Bryan slept in his bassinet right next to us. I am so grateful Mam-Maw let us move in with her.

I admit, life wasn't turning out as I had planned. I didn't know how long I'd live here. Or where I'd go to live next. Or how I'd continue to pay for the things my babies needed. But I knew one thing for sure: No one was going to take my beautiful babies away from me! I would find another job and I would provide everything my babies needed, no matter what.

My love for these two little boys God had entrusted me with grew with each breath I took. Joshua, with his head full of golden-brown curls, his beautiful smile, and the obvious love he had for me, his mama. Joshua and I both loved his little brother who was only a few days old. I loved giving Joshua kisses as I fed my sweet little baby Bryan, whose soft strawberry-red hair lay against my arm. No, I wasn't afraid right now. I was determined!

I was trusting God to provide for me and my little family.

I was trusting God to guide me.

God had taken me this far in my life, so there was no need to start doubting him now.

My main mission in life as I sat there on the sofa with my two young sons, not knowing what lay ahead for us, was that no matter what, they would always feel loved and wanted.

At this moment in my life, my prayer was that my boys would never feel "less than." My boys would never feel invisible. I hoped and prayed they felt my love from the inside out, every minute of every day. One day, they would know the love of God as well, and I silently prayed for God's protection over them always.

I had to find a job and get back to work soon. I had to start buying more diapers and food or God only knew how long we were going to make it.

My mother was bartending at a small, dark, smoke-filled bar off of East Lancaster near downtown Fort Worth. Mother said that she could get me a job there and I thought, *Why not?*

It seemed like a good idea because I could take care of the boys during the day and work at night. I'd be away from my babies during their waking hours the least amount of time as possible. Mam-Maw agreed to watch over Joshua during the nights. But she was too crippled to keep Bryan, so I paid my next-door neighbor to watch Bryan while I worked in the evenings. He was only ten days old when I started this new job bartending six nights a week at the Century 21 Club.

There I was standing behind the fifteen-foot long bar in an ugly dark, smoke-filled bar room. Looking out from the bar, I could see all of its ten little tables with four peeling brown fake-leather chairs around each table. The room's floor was covered with a filthy carpet that held on to the cigarette and cigar smoke, the smell of old spilled beer, as well as the chewing tobacco spit. There were men playing pool at the one pool table as smoke spiraled out of the big glass ashtrays sitting on each table.

The smell of the smoke and old beer lined my nostrils as I filled another cold beer mug. The sound of loud country music playing from the old jukebox filled the small bar room. People were both laughing and cussing.

I still remember thinking every night, *I sure don't know how I ended up here.*

It was a little bit funny for me to be a bartender because I didn't drink. I still don't drink! I had a few sips of some drinks in my early years, but I never liked the taste or had the desire. I don't smoke either, although I breathed in enough secondhand smoke during my short bartending career to last me a lifetime.

When I was pregnant with Bryan, I was the bartender at another bar, I would see beautiful women come in. I admired them. Oh, how I wanted to be like them, looking pretty and having fun. But by the end of the night, I knew I didn't want to be like them at all. They would sit there drunk, a cigarette hanging out of their lips, their once beautiful hair a mess and words slurring.

At closing time every evening, I'd look back at these same women and say a prayer to myself, "No, I'm pretty sure I don't want to end up like that."

I knew God had more planned for me to do with my life, and for my boys, if they wanted it.

I was having a little bit of trouble figuring out how to get there from here though. But for now, I was grateful for this hole-in-the-wall dumpy bar, with its big neon sign lighting up the front door and pay-by-the-hour motel rooms attached. The clients at the bar were a mix of contractors, businessmen, and blue-collar workers. We had a big group of regular customers. And for the most part, everyone was very nice. And I was going to earn a regular paycheck to buy the essentials my boys and I needed.

This was not exactly what I would call my dream job at my dream location, but it would put diapers on my babies and some food on the table. For now, this was all I knew how to do. I thought I was doing the best thing for my babies by taking this job.

I might not have gotten much sleep working all night, but I was physically and emotionally there with my sons every day until nearly bedtime. Hopefully soon, I would have enough money to move my little family into a small apartment of our own.

I had worked in the dark, stinky little bar only four nights when I thought, *Surely God had answered my prayers.*

There he was. A handsome six-foot-tall cowboy flashing his big pearly white smile at me from under his full head of thick brown hair and big hazel eyes. He was wearing starched jeans, a Western shirt, and ostrich boots. As he strolled across the floor toward the bar, he couldn't seem to take his eyes off of me. Or me off of him.

Now, with the benefit of 20/20 hindsight, I know better. Little did I know at nineteen years old, this man was not at all what God had waiting for me. I didn't have the wisdom to see the warning signs that clearly made me see the difference between his love and control over me.

(Ladies, a little warning: Take the time to make sure what you think is from God is really from God and not wishful thinking. The devil hides in sheep's clothing.)

It was my mother who introduced us; as far as she knew, Jack was a good guy. Everyone in the bar knew him and seemed to like and respect him. They shook his hands and bought him beers. He returned the favor and bought them beers too. All the women flirted with him. Yet somehow, all he seemed interested in was me.

He stood at the bar all night while I made drinks and waited on tables. He stood there until two o'clock in the morning. Closing time came and he was still standing there while I cleaned up the bar. All through the night as I worked, even when he was playing pool, I could feel his eyes on me. When I looked up, sure enough he was staring right at me. I could not believe he was interested in me because he could have any woman in the bar.

"Why me?" I wondered, feeling excited and flattered.

When I was done with my work, I told him he had to leave. I needed to lock up. But he insisted on staying and making sure I got out to my car safely.

"It's a rough neighborhood" was his explanation.

That was true. It was a rough area. Jack and a few other regulars stayed until I was done and escorted me out. This group always invited me to breakfast after closing, but the first few times I went straight home instead.

"My baby boys are at home, and they need me to be there when they wake up," I'd politely explain.

After turning down a few early-morning breakfast invitations, I realized my sons were fast asleep at that predawn hour of the morning, so why not go out and unwind? That's when I started joining Jack and the rest of the group for breakfast.

Night after night, Jack came into the bar; he was quite protective of me. He wouldn't let any of the other men near me. He had laid his claim on me. At this time in my life, I thought he was acting very romantic. Throughout the years since then, I've learned what I thought was romantic and love was actually all about control.

Looking back, I know it is important to know the difference in love and control as a young girl because it was very easy to confuse the two (love and control), especially when someone like me was hungry for love and attention. Seeing myself through Jack's eyes meant I would no longer be invisible.

How I wanted someone to love me and my boys. I wanted the perfect little family, or at least how I thought "perfect family" looked like at the time. I wanted to be the perfect wife, cook three meals a day, bake cookies, give my babies a bath each night, say prayers with them, and tuck them into bed each night. I pictured in my own imagination how on Sunday mornings all of us would walk into church in our Sunday's best clothes just like my Paw-Paw did with me. We'd sit together listening to God's Word. Then we'd go home and have a real sit-down family dinner together with plenty of food and of course a special homemade dessert.

Oh, how I wished for a complete family to love and take care of like this.

I imagined a husband who would hold me when he came home each night and make me feel safe and wanted. I felt so invisible that I might not ever find anyone who would want me or love me like this.

My first husband had an affair on me, which caused the divorce, even though I fought for the marriage. After that, all of the feelings of being unwanted, unlovable, and invisible from my childhood came rushing back, including the fact that no matter how good I tried to be, I was just never enough.

I was very confused because the previous man married me and said he would love me forever, but he turned away and found love from another woman instead. But now, here was this man standing in front of me who could have any woman. Instead, he was attracted to me in a powerful way. His attention made me feel wanted, loveable, and invincible.

When I looked into Jack's eyes, I felt deep down inside of myself like there must be something special about me. Why else would he be here night after night telling me how beautiful I was. He was constantly telling me, "You don't belong working in a dark, smoke-filled bar with a bunch of drunks."

Heck, I didn't think I belonged here either, but it was the way I could make a living to support my family. I desperately wanted to believe every word he said and every promise he made.

Now after about six weeks, we had fallen into a pattern. I was his girl, and he made sure everyone knew that. At that time, I was proud he claimed ownership of me. His attention made me feel special. It gave me hope that I might be loved.

Bryan was about six weeks old now. I had saved enough money to get us a two-bedroom apartment. Not long after I moved into it, Jack suggested he move in with me.

Why not? I thought.

"I'll help pay the bills," he said. "After all, we are together all the time anyway."

He seemed to love my boys, and it was important to me that his parents seemed to like me. Maybe this was the answer to helping me fix my life, because his family looked so normal. His parents had been married more than twenty years. He had family get-togethers regularly with his aunts and uncles.

I had met most of his family, and they were some of the sweetest and accepting people I had ever met. His aunt and mom started helping me out by keeping the kids while we were at work. His cousins, who were a few years younger than me, liked and loved me, and I loved them. Yes, this was a dream come true.

Could this be the family I had longed for and dreamed of all my life?

The next thing I knew, I was not feeling so well.

I was pregnant again.

Chapter 17

Despite The Warning Signs

Love is not blind, but it leads to blindness.
—Auliq Ice

It wasn't even a question if we would get married. Because after all, in those days, that was what you did when this sort of thing happened.

Besides, we were in love.

I can tell you from experience: Things that look pretty and perfect from the outside aren't always what they seem on the inside. Looking back, I can tell you the signs of abuse were staring me right in the face the whole time, but my definition of love and need for love clouded everything else.

I just didn't know what "true love" really looked like or felt like.

Not long after we moved in together, Jack started throwing things when he got mad, but I married him anyway because I was pregnant.

Not long after we moved in together, Jack started blaming things on me and terrorizing me until I gave him the money I had hidden to pay for the bills and food. Here I was pregnant again and this was happening, but I married him anyway.

Why? Because I kept telling myself, "It must be me. It must be my fault."

The family who raised Jack seemed normal, therefore he must have been raised with a proper upbringing, so it must be something I was doing wrong that made him act like this.

*****

Reasons Victims May Think They Can't Leave Abusive Partners

- Overall fear
- Children
- Lack of money
- Love of partner
- Children love both parents
- Law enforcement will blame the victim
- Clergy will blame the victim
- Relatives will blame the victim
- Victim blames herself/himself
- The batterer blames the victim
- Victim is a drug addict
- The partner is a pimp
- Victim's father was abusive
- Victim's mother was abusive
- Partner is an alcoholic
- Partner is a drug addict
- Abuser says, "I'm sorry"
- Abuser says, "I love you"
- Abuser says, "I'll never do it again"
- Abuser threatens, "I'll take the children"
- Abuser threatens, "I'll kill myself if you leave"
- Fear of losing custody of children if victim leaves
- Victim is deaf
- Victim is blind
- Victim is mentally impaired
- Victim can't read
- Victim is physically handicapped like in a wheelchair
- Victim can't speak English

- Victim doesn't have proper papers to be in country legally
- Victim assumes shelters are all full
- Victim fears becoming homeless
- Victim fears no one will believe her/his story
- Victim fears the welfare system will be more abusive
- Victim is already isolated
- Victim is depressed
- Victim never told anyone about the abuse before
- Victim is afraid of the unknown
- Victim is a public figure
- Abuser is a public figure
- Abuser is personal attendant/caregiver
- Victim feels there is no help
- Victim has tried to get help before
- Abuser found victim after leaving before

Chapter 18

Unimaginable New Life

*Be strong and courageous. Do not be afraid
or terrified because of them, for the Lord your
God goes with you; he will never leave you nor
forsake you.*

—Deuteronomy 31:6

It wasn't long before Jack was forcing me into the car and making me drive to the drug houses with him. I really didn't understand all that was going on with him at the time. Later I found out he had been using drugs the whole time we were dating, but he had done a good job of hiding it from me.

I never knew anyone who used hard drugs before, and didn't have any idea of what warning signs to look for.

After he got his drug fix, he would be nice and tell me how sorry he was. He'd tell me how much he loved me. He'd explain that he just needed to feel better.

I see now how this soon became a pattern in our life.

He'd always promise, "I'll never to do it again." The "it" began referring to his excessive drug use, stealing my money, hitting me, screaming at me, and the list goes on.

Little did I know at the time that the coming thirteen-year nightmare and roller coaster had just begun! How I wish I had seen or known how to get off this painful ride sooner. But I was so hopeful, so in love, and after all, our new baby was due any day now.

Surely the birth of his baby would change him?

I was hoping for a little girl to complete our family, but I didn't really think I would have one. I already had two boys, so I was pretty sure that this baby was going to be another little boy. I knew I would love this baby no matter what and had added him (or her) to my prayers long before we ever met face-to-face.

It was a hot morning on July 18, 1981. Our baby was due any day now. I fixed the boys breakfast. Bryan was seventeen months old, and Joshua had just turned three years old in March.

I was having some pains in my lower back but wasn't sure I was in labor. I told Jack what I was feeling, and he decided to go get a haircut.

We only had one car and he took it.

"Jack, I might be in labor, so please come right back," I said.

I went about my morning cleaning in the apartment and was loading the dishwasher when a pain shot through me. There was no doubt now I was in labor.

"Where was he?" I wondered.

It had been more than two hours since he'd left for his haircut.

Another pain, "Oh crap, I'm in trouble."

I was on the second floor of the apartment building. We had no phone. I had two babies I couldn't just walk out on. Bryan was sleeping in the baby bed, so my only option was to leave the door open so I could hear Bryan if he woke up. I decided to take Josh's hand and walk him down the stairs with me to the neighbor's and see if she would let me use her phone.

I knocked on her door.

No answer.

I went to the next, next-door neighbor.

No answer.

I was beginning to panic now.

I was starting to really hurt. Contractions were building. Bryan was asleep upstairs by himself. I had my other son in tow. I was stuck until I could find someone to help me.

I knocked on the next door I came to down the hallway, even though I didn't know the person who might answer the door.

To my relief, a lady did answer the door.

She had a phone and let me use it. Then she sent her twelve-year-old daughter upstairs to get Bryan and carry him down. I felt like we were going to be okay now.

I called my mother at work, but she didn't have a car there. She ended up borrowing a customer's car and came over to get me. She said, "I bet I know where Jack is. Do you think you can hold on if we stop to pick him up?"

Sure enough, he was drinking at a bar along the route to the hospital. Mother ran in and got him. Then off to the hospital we went. Not long after we arrived, my beautiful baby girl was born, weighing in at eight pounds and 9 3/4 ounces! She had a head full of dark brown, nearly black hair. Funny how that hair would turn as blond as cotton by the time she was a year old.

I couldn't believe it!

A perfect, healthy, beautiful baby girl! I counted her little fingers and her little toes. I held her tight.

My life was full and complete! God had blessed me with a baby girl!

To this day, I think they forgot to cut the cord because through everything we have both been through, we have always remained close. However, the same might be said about each one of my children.

The bond I had with my brother and sister was strong and unbreakable, but it still could not compare to the bond I had with my three children. I was determined they would have a better life than me, that they would never feel invisible if I could help it. I promised each one of them that and wrote it deep down inside my heart and soul. I thanked God. I asked him to help me keep my promise to my children.

Yes, I prayed to be able to provide my children material things, but if nothing else they would always feel loved and wanted because despite my best intentions, I had no way of knowing the train wreck that lay ahead of us.

The one thing I got right out of all of this was making sure my kids knew the Lord. Each one of us would come to need him more as the years unfolded before us.

By the time Tiffany was a year old, Jack was trying to get clean again. There was a place in Arizona that was supposed to be a Christian rehabilitation center. We could all go as a family and live there while Jack sought the help he needed. I will never forget the day his parents drove up to our house. We loaded the few things we were allowed to take with us into the car. The children and I got in Jack's dad's back seat. Jack was already there.

We were about to drive away from my home when a sick feeling came over me. I told Jack's dad, "Please stop. I don't want to go."

But his dad told me, "It's your duty. As his wife, you have to go be with him, to stand beside him no matter what. You can't just leave him out there alone."

I had made so many mistakes in my life up to this point, I thought he must know best. So I went.

It was years later when I realized it was never in the best interest of me that his parents cared about. No, for them, it was always about what Jack wanted or needed, and what would keep him out of their way.

We arrived in Arizona at an old motel that was turned into living quarters for the people at this facility. Each family had one room with double beds. I put Tiffany's baby bed at the foot of our bed. It was a tiny, cramped room, with a small bathtub and bathroom. They must have controlled the amount of hot water we could use because the bathtub would only fill about one-third full before we ran out of hot water.

We arrived in the wintertime, and the main thing I remember was I was always cold—freezing cold.

All meals had to be eaten with the rest of the group in the main dining hall.

I believe now, at least I'm pretty sure, we had gotten involved with a cult!

As my part in this, I had to wait tables in the restaurant that was open to the public and turn my tips over to the organization. I received no pay for my work, but was given a small stipend I could use at the store for extra toilet paper and necessities.

We were not allowed phone privileges at the facility, so after a few months of this, I snuck off the property and found a neighboring house to borrow the telephone. I called my mom and grandmother, who wired us three bus tickets to come home. I called Joshua's dad. He and his mother came that night and got the two boys out until Jack, Tiffany, and I could get away.

They drove all night and I got the boys out.

Tiffany wouldn't leave me, so Jack, Tiffany, and myself stayed at the neighbors' until it was time for the bus.

Jack even knew we were in a mess and he wanted out. The only thing good about those few months was I wasn't getting hit or threatened by Jack because he wasn't using drugs.

The facility did have church services there. However, I knew in my spirit this wasn't from God. I had known God as far back as I could remember, and his Holy Spirit was not there in that place. While I knew he was with us, I was sure what was going on there was not at all from the Lord. It was not God's voice speaking through the man at the front who was up there teaching. This realization scared me more than Jack ever did.

My Mother Margie in her wedding Dress
the day she married my father

Me at 10 months old

My father Peary Brock

Me and my sister Deby

One of our joint summer birthday parties under
our grandparents carport on Walthall

Peary, Deby, myself with cousins, Larry and Robbie

Mamaw and Pawpaw going to church - Jean and Jake Roden

Me and pawpaw

Part 3

Becoming
Invincible

Chapter 19

Changing a Destructive Legacy

Instead of your shame you sill receive a double portion, and instead of disgrace you will rejoice in you inheritance. And so you will inherit a double portion in your land, and everlasting joy will be yours.

—Isaiah 61:7

After we were finally set free from the fear, control, and abuse, I did what I was used to doing. I turned our apartment into our new home. A safe home. I became involved with all the children's activities at school. I worked at a job where I felt respected and appreciated. I cooked dinner for my family every night.

I tried hard to create the life I had always hoped for.

For better or worse, once we escaped, in my head, the horror, the fear, the pain were all in the past. We never discussed the past. We never talked about not discussing the past.

I just went silent and moved forward with our lives as if nothing had ever happened. After all, again, it was the past. Why look back on it? It was hard enough the first time around.

The biggest regret I have to this day was going silent after the escape.

I didn't know I was supposed to talk about it or get any therapy for me or my children.

No, I felt strong and confident, so we just plowed right on into the next chapter of our lives without taking the time to think, feel, or heal from the past.

I thought this was the best thing to do. I prayed I was doing the right thing and being a great mother. I was rebuilding our lives and trying to find what I thought was "a new normal" in the aftermath of it all.

For thirteen years, I was silent about the abuse, trying to protect and save my family. My focus was keeping us all alive. When that was done, I moved on. In my mind, I thought silence meant safety. I had no way of knowing at the time that I was passing down a very dangerous legacy that came close to costing my daughter her life as well.

It was several years later when I saw what my silence actually cost my little girl.

I was the strongest and most important person in my daughter's life. Tiffany saw me as a powerhouse role model. In her eyes, there was nothing in the world that could stop her mom. Tiffany admired me, looked up to me, and thought I had all the answers.

Well, if in Tiffany's mind, this was all true, and her mother allowed a man to abuse her. If her mother didn't value herself, then Tiffany felt somewhere deep in her mind that abuse and violence were all just a "normal" part of any relationship.

Sadly, it would be years later until I knew what I had unintentionally done. All those years, I kept silent in order to keep everyone safe. However, the silence would come back to haunt me in the years to come.

Tiffany was in a relationship with a young man. She was in high school and only seventeen years old. The relationship was just a young love, teenage relationship. I never saw the red flags.

You would think I would know the warning signs after years of abuse myself. But I had never taken the time to stop and process my life long enough to know there were red flags for me all those years ago and now for my little girl.

By the time this relationship ended, my daughter was beaten in the head with a hammer by her boyfriend while another girl held her down. A neighbor heard Tiffany screaming and called 911. That phone call was what saved her life. The young man spent several years in prison for this attack.

It would take years before I could forgive the man who did this to my little girl. And even longer for me to forgive myself. My heart is breaking as I write these pages as if this just happened today to my baby girl.

My heart can handle and use what happened to me, but my child? No, that will haunt me for the rest of my life.

I can still hear the screams from the 911 call as these two high school kids were beating my daughter. The detectives played the recording for me to hear both before and during the trial.

What had gone wrong? I had tried so hard to protect her.

"Please, God, not my little girl! Not my little girl!"

This could not be undone, unheard, or unfelt. How would life ever be right?

What did I miss?

This could not possibly be happening to my Tiffany. Her life was supposed to be happy, joyful, full of hope, and safe.

I had no way of knowing at that time that this moment would be what caused me years later to break my silence. To shout from the mountaintops if need be about how wrong domestic violence is. To proclaim to the world if need be that I survived and escaped and so can you, so can your loved one! As long as I live, I will be the voice for those who can't speak up for themselves. I will work to save lives and educate others about the widespread impact of domestic violence and how to stop it.

No, I could not change what had happened to me or what happened to my beautiful daughter. But it did cause me to stop and look back to see what had gone so wrong.

It was time for me to face my past, to look at it straight on with God right by my side. I was able to look back at the haunted little girl who looked like me, and I grew up not knowing she had any value. The frightened but confident woman, the brokenhearted mother—all these titles were part of me; it became what defined me and gave me my why in life!

I prayed to find some way for God to help me forgive but not forget. But even more than that, to give me his power and authority to break the silence, to make a change, and to make an impact for his children.

I had to give God each hurt and allow him to fill those spots with his unconditional love. The hardest part was learning and accepting that I had to learn to forgive myself as part of this process too. I prayed that God would guide me in order to move forward and not let the past define my future any longer. I learned that my circumstances were just that: circumstance I was in, but not a part of who I am.

Circumstances were not who I was or what God said I was.

I know beyond a shadow of a doubt that my identity is in Christ Jesus, not in any man. Now that God has restored my life, and I am able to see my past with clearer vision, God told me it was time to be a voice. No more silence! Now without question, I know what God has called me to do.

God opened my eyes to see how I passed down a very dangerous legacy, one that was passed down to me and passed down to my mother and her mother as well.

That's the very definition of what a legacy is! The legacy of silence around domestic violence was repeated from generation to generation in my family tree.

It's not surprising actually. Women used to be property. There were no laws against violence toward women, and when I escaped, we were just starting to get human rights and legal rights as women and as wives in 1993.

I am so grateful we have stronger laws in place now and we are starting to see action taken against violent abusers and protection for the victims.

No, I could not change my past nor my daughter's, but God could use me to impact future generations. A legacy of silence is not what I will leave behind for my grandchildren and future generations!

My family's legacy of domestic violence ends here. It ends with me and my daughter and our healing. God showed me by allowing him to heal me and forgive me, that I was to use all this pain and all these trials in my life to help others.

God was clear with me about his hand in my mission. I am a victim's advocate.

God is in the business of restoring lives. He restored my life. He wants to restore your life and that of any friend or family members we can guide to safety as well.

My life and message stands on Genesis 50:20: "You intended to harm me, but God intended it for good. What is now being done. The saving of many lives."

God told me I would be:

> *The face for all victims who cannot be seen. The voice for all victims who can no longer be heard. And the whisper in the ear of all victims who still have a chance to run.*
>
> —Dawn D. Milson

I am begging you to get out and get help! Twenty people are physically abused by a loved one every minute of every day in the United States alone. This is more than 10 million victims of domestic violence each year. And these are just the cases reported.

One in three women will become victims of domestic violence. One in four men will become domestic violence victims as well. Sadly, again, these are just the numbers reported. The statistics would be much higher if all cases were reported.

Chapter 20

A Gift for Moving Past the Past

The light shines in the darkness, and the darkness has not overcome it.

—John 1:5

As I come to a close while writing this book, I have to reflect back to see how far God has brought me. Writing this book was not in any way easy. I have revisited times in my life I had wished I never had to live through the first time, much less go open the wound again and again. I have relived pain, grief, shame, and much heartache. I have once again faced my fears and faults, but once again taken time to thank God for my faith and his protection while on this journey.

Several times during the writing of the first two sections of this book, I didn't know if I could go on. I cried. I prayed. I begged God to please tell me for sure if this assignment was from him. While writing these sections, the pain was so great, there was a time I thought that I might have to seek medical attention.

I remember crying in the shower one night and asking, "God, if you really are calling me to do this, why is there so much pain? Why was this so hard?"

And then God reminded me of my why.

Through God's grace, we had made it out to safety.

We were blessed to have overcome the violence and abuse.

During each and every trial, God had seen us through. No matter how many times I fell down, God kept extending his mercy, his love, his grace, and his protection. No matter what happened, he would reach right back down and lovingly pick us up again.

I fought myself on writing this book and putting my story out there more than once during this process. The more I wrote, the more I realized what a hot mess my life really was. I wasn't quite sure how I could have taken so many wrong turns in my life, when I was trying from the time I can remember to create a good one!

No, I thought, how can I put all this on display?

To everyone reading this book, you are seeing into places in my life and reading things I have never told anyone but God before now.

I knew he would not judge me, but I wasn't too confident about the rest of the world. What harm might this do to my family and the judgments against them? I questioned. So again, I hesitated.

I felt God was clear about what he wanted from me. But this was still going to get very hard. I was questioning, not God necessarily, but my ability to do what God wanted from me.

Every time I faltered, God showed up for me. More times than I can explain. But still, I worried. Then there was a moment that came in my life during the completion of this book that made me know for sure, removed all worry, and made me exclaim: "I will not hesitate again! Without a doubt, this book will be written *and* published! Nothing and no one would stop me."

Here's the story of how God made it clear for me to take the risk and not turn away from finishing this book. He made my "why" very clear once again!

One Saturday afternoon, while sitting around and visiting with my daughter, she casually asked: "Mom, how's the book going for you? Are you getting close to finishing it?"

I looked my thirty-seven-year-old daughter in the eyes, watching for any hesitation or concern. "Yes, I am getting very close to finished."

She sat back for a moment before she said, "Okay, Mom, you better tell me some more about this book."

I hesitated because we were having such a good conversation, and I didn't want to do anything to upset this good time together. I wasn't sure how bringing up the topic of this book could lift up her spirits, or if it might hurt her. Tiffany had known the basis of this book because I had asked each one of my children ahead of time for their approval about me writing this book. Because not only was my life being exposed, so were their lives. Each one of them had given me their blessing. However, until I started putting the story on paper, none of them knew for sure how far and how deep God would ask me to dig in order to bring about healing for others.

I took a deep breath, leaned toward Tiffany, and said, "You know this book is about the things that your dad did to me, right?"

No response. No reaction.

"I just want you to know that this book is not written in hatred or as revenge. I have forgiven him. I'm writing this story to bring about change and help other victims know there is a way out. I want others to know there is always a way to escape. And there is a way to start over. That God has more planned for them, nothing is impossible for them."

Tiffany stopped me.

She leaned over and grabbed my hand and said, "Mom, you know Dad loved you, don't you?"

I started to respond with my normal answer that I had given her for the past twenty-five years, which was, "Yes, Tiffany, I know your Dad loved me." This answer was meant to protect her from the truth and from any pain. It was meant to not talk bad about her dad. Not that this strategy had served either one of us well over the years. But old habits die hard is what the old saying is.

This time, as I started to open my mouth to say those same old empty reassurances, I was stopped. I believe it was the Holy Spirit. I had to take a deep breath. Then I was overcome with the need to speak these truths for the first time in our lives.

I asked Tiffany two questions:

First, "Tiffany could you ever imagine *me* beating *you?*"

She looked at me appalled and said, "No, Mom. Not ever!"

Second, "Tiffany could *you* ever imagine beating *me?*"

Again, she looked at me with a hard, consistent stare. She said, "No, Mom, I would never do that!"

I looked back at her beautiful eyes and replied, "Do you know the reason why I wouldn't be able to beat you or why you wouldn't beat me?"

She just stared at me but didn't answer. I said, "Because I know you love me and I love you. Love doesn't hurt."

All of a sudden, I could see a shifting light grow inside her. A new understanding of what love is and isn't.

She just kept looking at me. I knew she was thinking about what I'd said. I knew there was a huge moment of recognition. For the first time in her life, she understood what love looked like for sure.

I said, "Tiffany, there is a very fine line between love and control. Control can look a whole lot like love when you're wanting someone, anyone to love you. But when someone wants to know where you are every minute of every day…or when someone follows you everywhere to keep track of you…or gives you a time to be home or else…and uses physical abuse and fear to control you, that's not love."

As I watched her eyes slowly change with understanding, I knew our family legacy had changed as well. I was overcome with sadness because we had never had this conversation before, but so grateful that God had opened the doors for us to have it now.

I added, "All of this may feel like concern for your well-being, but that is an unhealthy level of control, not love. When someone says I would rather see you dead than let anyone else have you, that's not love. That is the difference between love and control."

She just sat there and listened, so I added, "Tiffany, love doesn't hurt. The hands and fists of a loved one do not cause pain or fear."

Once again, God affirmed in me how powerful a single voice can be. I was seeing firsthand that my voice matters.

The next words out of Tiffany's mouth were what made me know for sure that God had us in his hands and he was guiding this book. I felt like he was reassuring me that all would be well no matter what. She said, "Mom, I thought when somebody beat you, that meant they loved you."

I could not believe what I was hearing. I just looked at my daughter in shock.

After the shock began to settle, I said, "Tiffany, I am so sorry that you thought that."

I hesitated a moment and thought about her remark some more. Then added, "Tiffany, I think I can understand why you might think that. Tiffany, would you say I am the strongest woman you know?"

She responded, "Yes, Mother, you are!"

"And you saw me allow the beatings in my life, so did you think if someone as strong as me would allow this, it must be okay? And since your Dad said he loved me and then beat me, you thought that was normal?"

"Well, yes. I guess I did."

Wow! Really? Here I was speaking on domestic violence for more than eight years and never once did I realize that my own daughter didn't know the difference between control and love.

It broke my heart.

But then again, writing this book allowed us to break the silence and talk about the difference between love and control. Now, there is no doubt in my heart that she does know there is a difference. I knew in those moments that my little girl's heart was transformed. She will never, ever allow anyone else to hurt her again.

While I was contemplating that, Tiffany showed me exactly why this book must get written and the message must get out. She took a deep breath and said, "Mom, yes, your story and this book have got to go out."

We sat in silence, looked at each other, and realized that both of our lives had just taken a major turn. No matter what, both of us were dedicating our lives to reaching out and helping others to learn the difference between love and control. We both know God has great things in store for our lives, which is a lot more than what man may say we deserve.

As I was driving home from seeing my daughter, I was reflecting on our conversation, thinking how good God is and how I had a renewed determination for finishing this book.

Yes, God made it clear that my story in this book would be finished.

I was so excited in my spirit, so free, that when I returned home, I called my mother. I said, "Mom, I just got back from visiting Tiffany."

I told Mother about the conversation we had about the difference between control and love.

My seventy-eight-year-old mother paused and said nothing for a few seconds. Very unlike my mother.

She said, "Dawn, until you just voiced the difference between love and control, I did not know the difference either."

Really? My mother didn't understand the difference either?

Another sign about how important it is to share my story because women across generations need to know it is not their fault they fell victim to someone who was controlling them, not loving them.

God demonstrated to me over and over again how I need to be a voice for others and how we need to continue to reach out to one another and not just assume that each other knows what love really is. And also, there should be no judgment of others. Judgment is not love either.

Chapter 21

Finding Peace

You, dear children, are from God and have overcome them, because He who is in you is greater than the one who is in the world.
—1 John 4:4

Throughout my life, I cannot say peace was really a friend of mine. It always seemed to allude me, no matter how hard I chased after this feeling of peace everyone seemed to talk so fondly about.

I would look for it, pray for it, even beg God for it. Rearrange my life trying to find it.

After years of searching for this feeling called peace, the day finely came when I realized I had found that very thing: peace.

I found out peace was not something that could be bought or sought after. All those feelings of being unloved, unworthy, and never enough are not my identity; it is not who Jesus says I am.

> "See what great love the Father has lavished on us, that we should be called children of God! And that is what we are!" (1 John 3:1)

Peace started to show itself in my life when I realized my self-worth did not come from my circumstance, but from whom I am looking toward to handle my circumstance: Jesus Christ.

Peace was only found when my heart remembered to turn to God first to handle each and every situation in my life, no matter how big or how small.

I learned that whatever life throws my way now, peace is buried deep within my soul through our Lord Jesus Christ.

From the time I was a very small child, the feelings of shame, guilt, fear, and unworthiness attached themselves to me and only grew stronger as the years passed by. But the day finally came when I knew that I was no longer that scared, invisible little girl that always lived in fear.

I was no longer that victim who was nearly beaten to death.

No, I am not!

I am a survivor!

I am a child of the most-high God who has inherited the kingdom of heaven!

Through the years, God's Holy Spirit filled me and pieced back together a broken heart and shattered life, the shattered shell I lived in. I found out: "Fear would have to face the GOD I know" (Dawn D. Milson).

> "For God has not given us the spirit of fear, but of power and love and of sound mind" (2 Timothy 1:7).

Chapter 22

Journey with God's Word

"I will never leave you or forsake you."
—Joshua 1:5

No matter where you are on your journey in life, I put together this chapter as a quick reference guide of scriptures to refer back to when the lies of the enemy start creeping in. My prayers are that you start moving forward in the direction God leads you, which can look very different for each of us. God's Word is powerful and true, and we can always count on his guidance throughout our lives.

> For the word of God is alive and active. Sharper than any double-edged sword, it penetrates even to dividing soul and spirit, joints and marrow; it judges the thoughts and attitudes of the heart. (Hebrews 4:12)

I am at the point in my journey that I know with all my heart that God has:

- Replaced fear with courage.
- Replaced shame and guilt with self-respect and hope.
- Replaced rejection with love and acceptance.
- Replaced unworthiness with worthiness and value.

I no longer try and find my value in what other people think of me or any skill God has blessed me with. I have learned there is no person who can fill the emptiness in life other than Jesus Christ. He is the only one who truly loves without condition. He accepts each of us exactly where we are. His love is limitless. His grace is limitless. His protection is limitless.

I know his promises are as true for you as they are for me.

Fear

After reading my story, I am sure you have realized by now fear is something I am all too accustomed with. I am sure many of my readers are as well. Fear has a way of wrapping around each of us so tightly that breathing is hard and moving is hard. The thought that we may never know what life feels like without fear can add an extra layer of fear on top of fear.

It has taken me years to learn how not to live with fear as a constant companion. My prayer for you is that your journey with fear will be shortened as you plant the Word of God in your heart. It has been through much prayer and standing on the promises of God's Word that I have been able to break free of fear, which has released me to step into the call God has placed in my life.

When you feel fearful, please use one of these passages to hold on to until the fear passes:

- "Do not fear for I am with you, do not be dismayed for I am your God, I will strengthen you and help you; I will uphold you with my righteous right hand" (Isaiah 41:10).
- "For God has not given us a spirit of fear, but of power and of love and of a sound mind" (2 Timothy 1:7).
- "The Lord is on my side. I will not fear. What can man do to me?" (Psalm 118:6)
- "There is no fear in love. But perfect love cast out fear; because fear involves torment. But he who fears has not been made perfect in love" (1 John 4:18).
- "Be strong and courageous, do not be terrified; do not be discouraged for the Lord your God will be with you wherever you go" (Joshua 1:9).
- "The name of the Lord is a strong tower; the righteous run to it and are safe. Behold, God is my salvation, I will trust and not be afraid" (Proverbs 18:10).
- "For you did not review the Spirit of bondage again to fear, but you received the spirit of adoption by whom we cry out, 'Abba, Father'" (Romans 8:15).

"I sought the Lord, and he answered me: he delivered me from all my fears" (Psalm 34:4).

"God is our refuge and strength, an ever-present help in trouble" (Psalm 46:1).

Shame and Guilt

Feelings of guilt and shame just loved to eat me up from the inside out. I could actually write a whole book on these two emotions. I think shame and guilt were so much a part of my life, I had trouble setting them free. I didn't know how to feel without them!

The devil just loved for me to hang on to shame and guilt because they would stop me from fulfilling the purpose and plans God had for my life!

I do not care what you have done in the past, because once you have accepted Jesus Christ in your life, your sins are forgiven and they are covered by the blood of Jesus. Therefore, shame and guilt have no place in your life.

Much of the shame and guilt, we put on ourselves, and the world is all too happy to add on more. While you are not responsible for other people's actions, you should also not carry any shame and guilt with you regardless of where it comes from. You are who God says you are, and his words do not include shame and guilt to describe who you are. Remember, you are a child of the most-high God.

I will share with you, it is my experience that as I moved forward in my life and started standing on God's promises, shame and guilt kept trying creep over me again. Satan likes nothing more than to make me start doubting that I can overcome my past and try to keep me from moving forward in the purpose God created me for.

When you feel shame or guilt, please use one of these Bible passages to hold on to until these negative feelings pass:

- "For I know the plans I have for you declares the Lord plans to prosper you and not to harm you plans to give you hope and a future" (Jeremiah 29:11).
- "As far as the east is from the west so far has He removed our transgressions from us" (Psalms 103:12).
- "Instead of your shame you shall have double honor" (Isaiah 61:7).
- "If God is for us who can be against us" (Romans 8:31).

- "I took you from the ends of the earth from his farthest corners I called you, I said 'You are my servant I have chosen you and have not rejected you'" (Isaiah 41:9).
- "Those who look to him for help will be radiant with joy, no shadow of shame will darken their faces" (Psalms 34:5).
- "Therefore, if anyone is in Christ he is a new creation, the old has gone, the new has come" (2 Corinthians 5:17).

Rejection

Rejection is a feeling I experienced and felt at many different points in my life. Based on the title of this book, *Invisible to Invincible*. During so much of my life, I felt totally invisible, unworthy, and rejected. For most of my life, *invisible* was the keyword to describe me. *Invisible* is another word for *"rejected,"* based on how I felt from as far back as I can remember.

I felt rejection from my parents, friends, and society in general. As a matter of fact, many times while writing this book, I didn't want to share my past, partly for fear everyone in the world would reject me once again.

Fear of rejection is one reason there is so much secrecy surrounding domestic violence. Even years after a victim has escaped and moved forward in life, the fear of rejection keeps a strong hold. Often, the very thought that God would not reject me was at times hard to accept and believe. But I learned to take a stand on the following Scripture verses when the feelings of rejection start moving inside me. I remember: I am enough through Jesus Christ.

When you feel rejection, please use one of these passages to hold on to until the negative feelings pass:

- "The Lord will not reject his people he will not abandon his special possession" (Psalms 94:14).
- "Give all your worries and cares to God for He cares about you" (1 Peter 5:7).
- "Don't be afraid, you are more valuable to God than a whole flock of sparrows" (Matthew 10:31).
- "If the world hates you remember that it hated me first" (John 15:18).
- "Even if my father and mother abandoned me, the Lord will hold me close" (Psalms 27:10).

"He will listen to the prayers of the destitute. He will not reject their pleas" (Psalms 102:17).

"I can do all things through Christ who strengthens me" (Philippians 4:13).

Brokenhearted

To try to address a broken heart…hmmm, where to start? My heart has been shattered into so many pieces so many times throughout the years. There was a time I wasn't even sure if it would ever be whole again. I think when a heart is broken, the whole body feels broken. Time seems to stand still during these moments of brokenness.

When my heart was broken, I couldn't breathe, couldn't think clearly, a deep dark depression seemed to fall all over me and cast a shadow on me. There were times I wasn't sure if I wanted to take the next breath.

I highly encourage taking the next breath. A heart does mend. I know this to be true because I have experienced it. With God's help, the darkness will fade. Jesus Christ is the healer who can and will heal the brokenness and make the darkness fade away as the light of the Holy Spirit restores joy back into life.

Smiling again after this kind of healing is a real joy, a smile is no longer just be a facial expression for the world to see. After this type of healing a smile feels real from the inside out as God's peace and joy radiates throughout your whole being.

When you feel the pain of rejection, please use one of these Bible passages to hold on to until the pain and negative feelings pass:

- "He heals the brokenhearted and binds up their wounds" (Psalms 147:3).
- "Those who sow in tears shall reap in joy" (Psalms 126:5).
- "He is near to those who have a broken heart and saves those who are crushed in spirit" (Psalms 34:18–19).
- "Be kind and compassionate to one another forgiving each other just as in Christ God forgave you" (Ephesians 4:32).
- "And the peace of God which transcends all understanding will guard your hearts and your minds in Christ Jesus" (Philippians 4:7).
- "Now may the God of hope fill you with all joy and peace in believing That you may abound in hope by the power of the Holy Spirit" (Romans 15:13).

Chapter 23

Trusting in Love Again

There is no fear in love; but perfect love casts our fear, because fear involves torment. But he who fears has not been made perfect in love.
—1 John 4:18

On February 6, 1999, I took a leap of faith and married the true love of my life. He has been my rock. He has loved me and all three of my children through all the healing and other parts of our lives that have sometimes been messy and hard. Thanks to him, I have learned to love and trust again.

God's grace brought us together and it is through his eyes I began to learn and trust my discerning instincts that love was not defined by control.

Nick was my greatest advocate as the years passed. He was the one who encouraged me to move forward and fight for domestic abuse victims. After working a full-time job and then going home and staying up all night writing speeches or preparing to teach another class, he encouraged me. There were days I would be so exhausted, I couldn't remember my why.

I would say, "I can't do this. I'm not making any difference."

He would listen, hug me, and encourage me to get back to work.

I'd say, "I'm just want to quit. Am I really making a difference?"

He would lovingly touch my shoulder and say, "You know you won't stop. You're just tired. You know your why. Your story has to be told."

He has sacrificed his vacation time and free evenings to go with me and help me get ready for an event or speech. He has attended just about every speech I've made. I see him sitting in the crowd and think, *Now this is real love.*

He is not selfish with my time or his love.

He fights this battle against domestic violence by my side.

We have spent the last twenty-one years growing up together, and I can't image either one of us doing life without the other.

The point of this is to encourage you ladies, there are many good men out there—ones who know love does not hit or abuse or harm you in anyway.

Me and Nick on our wedding day

Joshua, me, Tiffany, Bryan

Joshua, mother, me, Tiffany, Bryan

Chapter 24

Becoming More Than Our Circumstances

When he had received the drink, Jesus said, "It is finished." With that, he bowed his head and gave up his spirit.

—John 19:30

I have gotten my happily ever after, thanks to being true to God's call for my life. I know not every day will be perfect or easy, but my faith will carry me through. And I am happy to say I have been blessed to watch my brothers and sister overcome their difficult circumstances as well.

My brother Peary was very mad when we were taken away from my mother's home. He was six years old and in first grade when we were pulled out of school in the middle of the year. Peary was practicing for a role he was chosen to do in the school play as a circus ringmaster. He was so proud the teacher had picked him for this part. But he never got to be the ringmaster because despite the fact that he had practiced for days and days, we were taken away before the play was done. As Peary grew up into a nice young man, he never forgot this disappointment. But I watched him take that role of ringmaster to heart. He became a real ringmaster in his own life. His performance in his own life is spectacular and has inspired me. Perry has grown from that hurting, brokenhearted little boy who was dealt a cruel hand, to a successful business owner and family man with a wife and two sons and grandchildren.

My sister Deby grew up to be a beautiful and smart young woman. She had a big heart and loved me like a mother, which sometimes she acted like, since she was fifteen months older than me. She should have never worried about being pretty enough or any of those other negative feelings she had as a small girl. When Deby was about twenty years old, she was in the Miss Texas pageant and made it to the finals. Deby ended up marrying a wonderful man and they had one daughter. In April 2012, Deby was diagnosed with a rare cancer and lived for only five months afterward. To this day, I am so glad she was able to see her daughter grow up to the age of twenty-five years old and graduate from Harvard. In many ways, Deby was the one who began to change the family legacy into something we could all love. Deby and her husband helped save my life when I needed them most. I know she loved me. As a matter of fact, I think God is showing me again just how much she was and still is a part of my life as I sit here telling her story on the sixth anniversary of her death.

Of all the hard things I had to deal with as a child, one of the biggest was leaving my half-brother behind with my father as the rest of us went back to live with Mother. But despite the distance that separated us, we have remained close. There is no amount of time apart or distance that will break our bond. Through the years, Kyle and I have stayed connected and close in good times and bad, to encourage each other no matter what. Kyle is a wonderful man as well. He owns his own successful business, is married, and has two grown daughters and a grandchild.

Then there is Hershel, my half-brother from my mother and stepfather. He is six years younger than me. He experienced the sadness and loss when we were taken away at the end of each summer to go back and live with my father during the school year. But we made the most of those summers and built bonds that would last throughout our lives. I will be forever grateful that he stood beside me, packing his pistol, as he played the role of bodyguard during my escape and many other times during my life. I never doubted that he would lay his life down for me if it ever came to that. He also ended up marrying and having six successful children and grandchildren of his own.

It can be said that looking back on each of our lives, there is one saying that my brother used to say was true for each one of us:

"Throw me to the wolves and I will come back leading the pack."

I tell you all this so you will see that we have worked hard to not be defined by our circumstance. Growing up, life tossed us around, but we overcame individually and together. We have been near destruction in our lives, but God has seen us through all of it.

Again, I tell you this so you will see it is all possible for you as well. Just reach out and God will provide the way. There is also help and hope for you. God always makes a way when there is no way.

Chapter 25

A Legacy Restored

Stand firm with the belt of truth buckled around your waist, with the breastplate of righteousness in place, and with your feet fitted with the readiness that comes from the gospel of peace, take up the shield of faith...take the helmet of salvation and the sword of the Spirit.
—Ephesians 6:14–17

God's grace never stops amazing me. When I look back on my life, I see grace each and every time I look in the mirror, with every breath I take. I look back and see God's grace sprinkle all throughout my life. By allowing God to restore each area in my life, I have been able to move forward in changing the legacy I want to leave behind for future generations: one of courage. I want to be known for staring fear right in the face, as I protect myself with the:

- Shield of Faith
- Belt of Truth
- Breastplate of Righteousness
- Shoes of Peace
- Helmet of Salvation
- Sword of the Spirit

I want to be remembered as a woman of great love—the kind of love God has shown me: a love for her family, friends, and God's people—who chose to break her silence and not be invincible any longer, but through the power of Jesus Christ, became invincible in order to change the legacy I leave behind for future generations.

My prayer for you as you move forward in your life is you will always feel God's hand of grace upon you. As the journey to heal begins, you may feel the journey is long, but I promise you it is worth fighting for. God will never leave your side. You can do this. Let the healing begin.

I pray by telling my story, it will encourage other victims to escape and find their voice as well.

May God bless each of you as the journey begins.

Chapter 26

Remember the Cotton

Then he said to his disciples, "The harvest is plentiful but the workers are few. Ask the Lord of the harvest, therefore, to send out workers into his harvest field."
—Matthew 9:37–38

Many times after I gave a speech on the subject of domestic violence, I had strangers come up to me and say, "Dawn, you need to write a book about your story." But I would smile and just say, "Thank you," and then never gave it much more thought other than "I don't know anything about writing a book." A few days later, I was struggling to write a short biography for an event where I was getting ready to speak, but couldn't find just the right word I was looking for. I went to a friend and coworker to ask for help finding that right word. At the end of the conversation, this woman said, "Dawn, you need to write a book about your story." Again, I said, "Thank you." And this time, I said out loud, "I don't know anything about how to write a book."

My boss just happened to be standing there and overheard the conversation. She said to me, "I just met someone who helps people write their books. I'm going to introduce you her. I'm going to give her your name and have her call you, because you do need to write your story, Dawn."

There were several different personal trials in my own life dealing with children, parents, and so many other things, but those stories are for other books. The personal trials experienced during the writing process of *Invisible to Invincible* made me believe that the enemy was working overtime to stop this book, but I became even more determined to keep moving forward. It was God's call I was answering.

In the middle of writing this book, I questioned if I could keep working on it. I was crying a lot and feeling broken again. I asked God, "Did you really call me to do this? If so, why is it so hard? Please make it clear that writing this book is really what you want me to do." I was begging him to show me why I was doing this again because, "I don't think I can do it anymore."

It was at this breaking point that God reminded me of a trial I experienced two years earlier.

*****

I was driving to Lubbock, Texas, tired, frustrated, overwhelmed, and dealing with yet another major personal crisis in my life. I'd already been driving for hours, and when I got to Lubbock, all I saw between me and the horizon was cotton. I said to God, "If you're going to make me do this horrible drive, why can't you give me something better to look at than all this cotton?"

"Really, God, there isn't even a place to stop to buy a Coke. Everywhere I look, there is nothing but cotton, cotton, cotton."

I was not feeling very godly, but not to be deterred by my bad mood, the Holy Spirit spoke to me, "Dawn, look at the cotton. Really. Slow down and look at the cotton."

I was in no mood to slow down because I had to be somewhere, and all the cotton was hard to miss, so I said out loud, "You haven't given me much choice. As far as I can see, there's nothing but cotton. So why are you asking me to do something so obvious?"

The second nudge from the Holy Spirit made me take a deep breath, slow down the car, really hear God's voice, and pay attention to what he was asking me to do, "Dawn, look at the cotton."

I slowed my car down. As I turned my head from left to right, as I looked in front of me and behind me, as far as my eyes could see, there was nothing but cotton and more cotton. But I still didn't know what God wanted from me, so I asked, "What does all this cotton mean?"

God spoke to me and showed me that each cotton ball represented a life that would be touched by my story.

This happened two years before I knew I would write a book. So I assumed maybe God meant I'd be speaking to a lot of people.

I was so tired and worn out and angry, but I looked up to the sky and said, "God, that is a lot of cotton; that's so many people. God, are you saying I'm going to be speaking until I'm ninety years old? I don't know if I can do that, God."

But at that moment, there was a peace that fell over me and I felt like maybe I was hearing him now. I laid my head on the steering wheel and said to God, "Okay, God, if that is what you're calling me to do, I'll do it."

*****

As the speaking part of my life began to blossom again, other personal trials started up again also. Two years had passed since talking to God on the drive to Lubbock and in the midst of all that cotton, when I received this calling. This is one of the most personal conversations with God that I have ever had. It was so powerful, it almost defies description.

After I had started writing the book, I was home alone in a dark house getting ready for bed. It was close to midnight, and I walked into the totally dark kitchen. The only light came from the refrigerator once I opened the door. I was thinking about what I had just written for the book when the Holy Spirit spoke to me, "Dawn, remember the cotton."

I froze and got cold chills all over my body. I looked up and said out loud, "It's the book!"

He said to me, "Yes, it's the book."

I know now that this book is part of the way I will touch all the lives God has planned for me to impact. So I know that anyone who reads this book is one of the pieces of cotton that God is harvesting for his kingdom.

As a reminder of God's message about the cotton, and the strength and importance of this calling, I have a piece of cotton sitting in a vase on my dresser, with a southern magnolia.

Chapter 27

Get Out, Get Help

To each one of us grace is given as Christ apportioned it. God's grace is for everyone who asks to receive it.

—Ephesians 4:7

In case the definition of what domestic violence is not clear, here is the official definition according to the National Coalition against Domestic Violence:

> Domestic violence is the willful intimidation, physical assault, battery, sexual assault, and/or other abusive behavior as part of a systematic pattern of power and control perpetrated by one intimate partner against another. It includes physical violence, sexual violence, threats, and emotional/psychological abuse. Physical violence is often accompanied by emotionally abusive and controlling behavior as part of a much larger, systematic pattern of dominance and control. Domestic violence can result in physical injury, psychological trauma, and even death.

Do you recognize yourself in any of the situations you've read in *Invisible to Invincible*?

Do you recognize your relationship you have read here?

Do you recognize a friend, neighbor, or loved one in any of the scenes you've read?

What legacy are you leaving behind?

Are you like my daughter and mother were? They never gave much thought to the difference between control and love, but now you find yourself in a relationship that is based on abusive, possessive control?

If you answer yes to any of these questions, I want to end this book by begging you, if you are in an abusive situation, please get out. Please get help. Pease find the courage to pick up the phone and make that first telephone call. This is the hardest part, but help is just that one phone call away.

You do deserve better! And even if you don't believe you do, get help. Let us help you and hold you up, get you to safety and protect you until you can see and do these things for yourself. There are people who are willing to help you find what we know as the real truth—you do deserve more than the abuse you're suffering now.

If you have a loved one, friend, coworker, or neighbor who is suffering through domestic abuse, please reach out to get help for them too. Please do not turn a blind eye or turn you back and say, "It's none of my business."

Please get help; there is so much available at no cost.

There is a safe way to get out. It all starts with breaking your silence. One phone call will set things in motion.

I do not care who you are—rich or poor, educated or not. It doesn't matter where you came from or what you do; you are of value to God and others. God wants to walk with you through your healing. You get to move past your past, all you have to do is ask.

Domestic Abuse Hotline Numbers

Are you experiencing domestic violence or know someone who is? Ask for help.

Call these 1-800 telephone numbers and get help.

Reach out to a trusted friend or loved one.
National Domestic Violence Hotline
800-799-7233
Elderly/Child Protective Services
800-252-5400
In case of an emergency, dial 9-1-1

You may feel like the journey is long, but I promise it is worth it.
God will never leave your side.
You can do this.
You deserve to live safely and in peace.
Make the call. Let the healing begin.

Mary Flores – Founder
Dawn D. Milson – Co-founder
Shelly Muncy- Co-founder

Author Dawn D. Milson

Contact Information

Website: DawnDMilson.Com
E-mail address: <u>Dawn@DawnDMilson.com</u>
Facebook: @TheRealSteelMagnoliaForgedByGrace
LinkedIn: Dawn D. Milson

Nick and Me at Mission Granbury Gala

About the Author

Dawn D. Milson is a survivor of domestic violence, victims advocate, and sought-after speaker. Dawn is also the cofounder of We've Had Enough Abuse, a community outreach program. Dawn works with her community's women shelter in order to raise funds and bring about change. Dawn's positive outlook in life spills over into joy that many say is contagious as her eyes light up and sparkle as she speaks of the mercy and grace God has shown her throughout her life. Dawn is in ministry and feels it is a privilege to serve others in order to bring them closer to Christ.

Dawn's passion in life is to help victims and others overcome, persevere, and flourish in their own lives, regardless of past or present circumstances. Through Jesus Christ.

Dawn's personal mission statement is "I will be the face for all victims who can't be seen, the voice for all victims who can no longer be heard, and the whisper in the ear of all victims who still have a chance to run."

Dawn is a wife, mother, and grandmother. She treasures her family time. Her grandchildren have become her greatest joy. Dawn loves decorating and cooking huge meals for the holidays! Her greatest desire for her family is to change a legacy of silence that has been passed down through many generations. Dawn and her husband have five dogs and two cats which are her constant companions. She loves animals and feels a need to rescue and feed animals and people. Dawn and her family reside in north Texas.

About the Coauthor

Arlene Gale is an international and national award-winning author and #1 best-selling author for her book *Face Forward Move Forward: The Journey to Discard a Painful Past and Determine a New Legacy of Peace and Possibilities*. Her most recently published book is her eighth, *Book Business Blueprint: Build Credibility, Stand Out from the Competition, and Skyrocket Sales by Writing Your Book*, which is earning great reviews from across the country.

Website: BookWritingBusiness.com